What Say YOU?

E. Eugene Williams, Ph.D.

What Say YOU?

E. Eugene Williams, Ph.D.

River City Press, Inc.
Life Changing Books

What Say You?

ISBN: 1-9343271-8-2

Graphic Layout:
Sara Jo Johnson
Roseville, MN

Published by:
River City Press, Inc.
4301 Emerson Avenue N.
Minneapolis, MN 55412
1-888-234-3559

DEDICATION

This book is dedicated to the Holy Trinity: God the Father, God the Son, and God the Holy Spirit for their presence, power, and purposes in my life. It is also dedicated with enduring love to Ruth, my caring, daring, and sharing partner in ministry, and my compassionate and discerning wife for more than sixty years in a relationship that grows and glows in God's wisdom and strength.

June 22, 2007

To Steve and Patsy:
We know that when tones are added to a melody, so that two or more notes are heard simultaneously, the result is harmony. You have brought great harmony to the total musical program at the Powder Springs First Baptist Church. We are most grateful.

Gene and Ruth Williams

ENDORSEMENTS

"Concise, convincing, conscience-raising—Gene Williams' new book is all these and much more. In 35 brief snapshots he gives us a look at life as he has seen it over more than eight decades. Packed with anecdotes which will morph easily into sermon or lecture illustrations, *What Say You?* is a great read for anyone interested in the world around us. It will increase your vocabulary, stimulate your thinking and make you laugh."

Dr. Kenn Gangel
Distinguished Professor Emeritus, Dallas Seminary
Scholar–in–Residence, Toccoa Falls College

"Gene Williams plays words like a jazz musician slides from high notes to low, with passionate emotion, and remarkably subtle precision. Weaving contrasting threads of thought drawn from a disparate collection of colorful characters, his pithy essays are both amusing and provocative, each and every one a delightful read."

Ron Mattocks
Founder and President, Mattocks & Associates

"Dr. Williams has the uncanny ability to delve deeper into the meaning of our common every-day expressions, and fortify them with Scripture. *What Say You?* contains a wealth of sound advice and counsel for those searching for meaning in our troubled world. This book is entertaining reading as well as instructive."

The Reverend H. Leroy Patterson
Former Chaplin, Wheaton College, Illinois

"*What Say You?* is a wise and witty anthology of stimulating essays that encourage the reader to respond to succinctly articulated principles for success in life and leadership.

Drawing from his exhaustive knowledge of the arts and sciences, and from his extensive acquaintance with people known around the world, Dr. Williams frames each principle with an engaging border of stories and vignettes. These serve to highlight each principle, focusing attention on its veracity and power to effect change.

This book will expand your thinking about the importance of listening, the nature of faith, the handling of paradoxes, the need for balance, and a universe of other topics as well. Its biblical wisdom set in the context of real-life situations cannot help but evoke your response to the author's continued challenge, *What Say You?*"

David G. Reese, Ph. D.
Vice President for Academic Affairs, Toccoa Falls College
Toccoa, GA

"I have read thoroughly *What Say You?* and feel honored to share my thoughts. This is an unusual blend of depth and breadth—depth of thought and application to our deepest longings, and breadth of outreach into every facet of life on 'Main Street.' Illustrations and insights come from every corner of life today and yesterday, and will stir your desire to answer the recurring question *What Say You?* You will be a better person when you finish."

V. Gilbert Beers, Ph. D., Th. D.
Former Editor, *Christianity Today* Magazine
Former President, Scripture Press Publications

"Amidst the clutter and confusion of our culture we all desperately need clarity and perspective…*What Say You?* not only compellingly reminds us of what is really important in life but also shows us how to make the most of the life we have been given…Thank you so much, Gene, for this inspiring road map!"

Dr. Crawford W. Loritts, Jr.
Sr. Pastor, Fellowship Bible Church
Roswell, GA

"*What Say You?*" is highly inspirational, highly informative, and very quotable. Thanks for all the research and recall that went into this. I would love to see it published and believe that many a thinker and writer will draw from it."

Dr. Ravi K. Zacharias, President
Ravi Zacharias International Ministries
Norcross, GA

"Dr. Gene Williams is a man who has been greatly used by God in a wide variety of ministries. Well-respected by those who know him, he is eagerly sought out for the unusual wisdom and insight he has gained in a life of biblical study and leadership. All of this shines through in his book *What Say You?* It is a most interesting read and one you'll thoroughly enjoy!"

Dr. Les Lofquist
IFCA International Executive Director

"In just thirty-five encapsulated chapters, Eugene Williams has enough nourishment and therapy for the souls of each of his readers to last a lifetime in his book, *What Say You?* In the tradition of the wisdom of the sages of yore, he refreshes the heart, mind, spirit, and the merriment of all readers, regardless of their station or position in life. I heartily recommend this book for its simple, yet profound, penetration into the mysteries of ordinary or anxiety-filled lives in this age of post-modernity. Here's what we say, "Right On!""

Dr. Walter C. Kaiser, Jr., President
Gordon-Conwell Theological Seminary
The Colman M. Mockler Distinguished Professor of Old Testament

"Take the stroll down the brightly-lit aisle of Gene Williams' display of words well said. *What Say You?* Provides a tool kit for how to say what you say-a book that belongs on the shelf of every Christian thinker. You neglect this treasure at your own peril."

Dr. Howard G. Hendricks
Distinguished Professor, Dallas Theological Seminary
Chairman, Center for Christian Leadership

"Dr. Williams is a skilled craftsman in handling the words of the English language. The chapters of his book are interesting, informative, and practical. I found myself looking forward to reading the next chapter. He has an intriguing way of holding interest. The research and historical data make the book a profitable resource."

Dr. Elwood Chipchase, President
Calvary Bible College & Theological Seminary

"Your book is most enjoyable, interesting, provocative, and delightful. All these synonyms apply. I particularly appreciated how you wove everyday occurrences and storied into biblical principles with a practical application toward the reader to ask *What Say You?* I heartily endorse it!"

John H. Stoll, Th. M., Ph. D.
Executive Director of ASK, Inc.

SIMPLY STATED: THANK YOU

Plutarch, ancient Greek biographer and historian, who many believe lived from 46 to 120 A.D., shortly after the days of the Lord Jesus Christ spent upon this earth, wrote: "The worship most acceptable to God comes from a thankful and cheerful heart. It is up to the true God to determine what worship is most acceptable to Him. However, the intrinsic value of a thankful heart and cheerful spirit must not be overlooked.

I am now 83 years old and that permits me the privilege of being thankful to many wonderful and generous persons.

I have what I consider to be the most wonderful person I have ever met for a wife. Her name is Ruth. Our love and respect for each other continues to grow with each passing year and we already have a marriage that has lasted over sixty years. We have two very find children: Roger and Virginia (Ginger). We have a special daughter-in-law and son-in-law that delights our hearts as well. In addition, we have four granddaughters and their husbands in our family. The greatest cause for thankfulness is that all those named love Jesus Christ as their Savior and Lord.

My professor and personal mentor at Pennsylvania State University, Dr. Robert E. Dengler, taught me to love the classics and how to think with precision. A second professor at PSU, Dr. Edwin Zoller, taught me the necessity of total honesty. My professor and mentor at Michigan State University, Dr. David Ralph, showed by example how to combine heart and personal warmth with the learning process. I am indebted to my teacher, the late Dr. C. S. Lewis of Oxford University, for his shared insights into asking meaningful questions and searching diligently for cogent answers.

The privilege of sitting under the instruction of many Bible teachers and pastors has been my good fortune. Two of those expositors of the Word of

God stand out. They are Dr. Arthur B. Whiting and Dr. Ralph Stoll.

I am deeply indebted to many hundreds of friends who have enriched my life greatly. Among them are those who have endorsed this book, and those who have edited and published it.

I also want to thank Mr. Bill O'Reilly of Fox News. He gave me the idea to challenge the readers of this book to think for themselves and to make those thoughts relevant. His oft-repeated by-line, "What Say You?", served as strong motivation to setting into motion personal challenges to the issues of life.

CONTENTS

FOREWORD

The culture in which we live is constantly changing and life itself is getting more complicated and stressful. To be successful at life and leadership at any level demands a person's time, talents, energy and patience. It can be physically, mentally, emotionally, and even spiritually draining. The bottom line is that we need all the help we can get to be successful at whatever it is that we are called to do—whether it is being a friend, mate, parent, worker, or the leader of the largest church or organization.

Most people want to do their best and produce valuable results though their labors. This is true of everyday people, of heroic and admired leaders, and of those men and women behind the scene, not in the lime-light, that make such a difference in communities and organizations around the world. The question that should be in all of our minds is: What do we need to consider in order to live happier and more productive lives?

What Say You? Is a great book if you want to improve your life and the influence you have in this world. If you don't care about maximizing your achievements, then maybe reading this book will motivate you to realize you should. Making the most of our lives is a key ingredient to living a happy and fulfilling life. This book can help us to achieve all that we possibly can.

Whenever you read a book or take advice from someone, you should recognize the source of the wisdom being presented. The insights in this book about life come from a person who has had a positive impact on people's lives for sixty years. Dr. Eugene Williams has been a powerful influencer in the lives of followers and leaders around the world. I know this personally as he has mentored, coached, and befriended me. His wise counsel and advice has made a major impact in my life as a college president bring about change to an organization over one hundred years old.

Dr. Williams has the educational and professional credentials that puts him in a world-class level of leadership. He has been a war hero, a university and seminary professor, a university chaplain, a worldwide lecturer, and the CEO of an international mission agency, just to name a few of his accomplishments. He is a profound thinker who studied under the great C. S. Lewis, and a man who is a dedicated Christian with a deep level of biblical knowledge.

What Say You? will give to you an intellectual adventure because it will encourage you to think, to question, to challenge, and to get involved with the subject under consideration. Each chapter asks the reader to give thoughtful consideration to what Dr. Williams believes is important for growth and development. The book is not only thought-provoking, it is succinct, and timely. I am most impressed with the book in that it is pragmatic and practical. The book is not just focused on what is theoretical, but it leads to shaping our actions, which in turn can bring about maximal achievement in life and leadership. The reader is able to take the insightful thoughts contained in this book and apply them to the unique experiences of his or her life. Read the book and you will be the judge and jury.

George D. Miller III, Ed. D.
President, Davis College

INTRODUCTION

C. S. Lewis in his *A Preface to Paradise Lost* wrote: "The first qualification for judging any piece of workmanship from a corkscrew to a cathedral is to know what it is, what it was intended to do, and how it was meant to be used."[1]

This is good advice and a guideline to insightful understanding. This book is designed to be an enjoyable mind-stretcher in keeping with Oliver Wendell Holmes' (1809-1894) observation that "Man's mind, once stretched by a new idea, never regains its original dimensions."[2] That's *what it is intended to do.*

The ancient Greeks used the word *arête* to describe courage, valor, integrity, excellence, and a few other good qualities, especially in their soldiers and athletes. I would hope that a little arête could be sprinkled on the pages of this book and that, in turn, it would enhance the reader's life for good which explains *how it was meant to be used.*

That leaves us with the need to describe *what it is.* This book, written in pithy form, deals with some commonplace expressions and some novel ideas in order to give perspective to life's opportunities for greater achievement. It is a series of brief analyses awaiting your interpretations and applications. Together let's give it our best shot.

---

[1] Lewis, C. S., *A Preface to Paradise Lost* (A galaxy Book). New York: Oxford University Press, 1961 (Chapter One – Epic Poetry, p.1)

[2] Holmes, Oliver Wendell, *Quotation by Author* by Michael Moncur's *Cynical Quotations*, #26186. Can be found on the Website.

ONE

"WHAT SAY YOU?"

It comes as no surprise that our relationships with one another depend on the effectiveness of shared meaning and understandings. These, in turn, depend upon our abilities to communicate. In the process, both verbal and nonverbal communication, play prominent roles demanding competence to succeed.

When Bill O'Reilly of television's Fox New poses the question, "What say you?", as he does frequently on his telecasts, he is emphasizing two very important communication qualities. They are the invitation for dialogue and the willingness to listen carefully. How well he succeeds in each instance is an evaluation best left to his audiences to determine.

The concept of communication skills opens a plethora of options from Adams' emphasis on attitudes to Zuckerman's categories of zonal areas of communication—all inclusive from A to Z.

However, as the radar scans the literary horizon, the blips emanating from the communication transponder will highlight O'Reilly's "factors" of interpersonal dialogue and listening with active intensity.

It is a well recognized fact that Ted Koppel, "Nightline" host, combines both of these skills with apparent ease. He maintains a delicate balance between attentive listening and incisive questioning to those he interviews.

How do you identify a genuine listener? It should be assumed that you go beyond Mark Twain's observation, "The first person in a conversation to draw a breath should be declared the listener." Listening is a lot like taking physical exercise. Everyone is in agreement that it is desirable but many find it difficult to do consistently.

Nehemiah of Old Testament fame said it well. Listening is "hearing with understanding" *(Nehemiah 8:2)*. Actually, listening is a complex process that takes into consideration alert hearing, focused attention, meaningful understanding, retrievable remembering, empathetic evaluating, and personalized responding.

Good listeners do more than listen to <u>respond</u>, they listen to <u>understand</u>. That's where <u>empathy</u>, the ability to see and feel experiences as the other person does, and <u>objectivity</u>, the quality of discernment, join hands as Ted Koppel demonstrates.

You may recall the Jerry Marcus quip, "I can't get off the phone, he won't stop listening."

When it comes to effective listening we need to pray "…and lead us not into temptation." The temptation to daydream, to be preoccupied with other thoughts, to harbor hostile feelings, to be suspicious or prejudiced, to fake listening, to be defensive, to jump to conclusions, and to thrive on interrupting the speaker are serious barriers to effective communication.

Effective listening is not an end in itself. It is a God-given means of reaching out to others in order to help meet their needs and expectations selflessly as release persons of caring concern.

And then there is the invitation to dialogue packaged in O'Reilly's "What say you?" This is an interpersonal matter primarily, although it can be a group thing as well. It is communication between or among connected persons, usually involved in either close or shared relationships. In fact, effective communication is at the heart of meaningful interpersonal relationships and that's where dialogue play such a prominent role.

Dialogues have come upon rough times in modern society. They might well have been buried in the graveyard of discussion techniques were it not for radio and television and stimulating personalities like Bill O'Reilly, Ted Koppel, Jay Leno, Barbara Walters, and others.

Dialogue is an ancient form of interpersonal communication. It was much more popular during America's Colonial Period. Today, it requires well-informed participants who are able to express their thoughts well, who segue from one concept to another with transitional smoothness, and who quit while the interest remains high.

Good dialogue is carefully planned but not rehearsed. It thrives on sharp wit, direct answers with "no spin" as O'Reilly advocates, with spontaneity, and with hot issues.

The questioner's job is to ask the right questions, in the right way, at the right time. The questioner assumes that he or she represents a larger audience as spokesperson. The respondent should be highly regarded for both integrity and knowledge ability. Honesty is needed.

There are real and threatening risks involved in dialogue which accounts for the number of "no shows" who decline invitations to appear when asked. In the midst of a world of great turmoil, trying to cope with tremendously important issues that require solid answers, all of us need the experience of living with people who speak and listen out of the depths of their beliefs and stand for them with courage. What say you?

TWO

"LETTER – HIGH"

Letter-high. This is more than an expression frequently emerging from the mouth of a play-by-play radio or television announcer in the realm of baseball. It is a standard of measurement.

Any pitch that crosses home plate above the letters on a player's uniform is out of the "strike zone" and it is called a "ball."

The question arises. Just how precise or accurate is this particular standard of measurement? Letter-high varies with the height of the ballplayer. The taller the player the higher from the ground will be the letters on his uniform.

Another variation is based on the umpire's concept of the "legitimate strike zone." The umpire, it is said, "calls 'em as he sees 'em" and this could change the standard of measurement. Is he generous with his call or does he hold a strict strike zone?

The player's stance at the plate enters into the equation. Does he stand erect or does he squat? If he squats, how far down does he lower the letters on his shirt as he does so?

S. I. Hayakawa, in his book entitled *Language in Thought and Action*, stressed misunderstandings based upon what he termed a "one word, one meaning fallacy."[1] This well-known semanticist touched a pressure point. Most words are equivocal, yielding to two or more possible interpretations. Some, in fact, have numerous interpretations as any dictionary verifies.

Hillary Rodham Clinton described her personal involvement as "minimal" in the Arkansas real estate scandal. What did "minimal" mean? If a large corporation "lays off" or "dismisses" 80,000 employees and calls it "downsizing" or perhaps "restructuring," how would you interpret this action?

It goes without contradiction that English is the most often used language in world history, being used by one out of every seven persons on earth. English has the most extensive vocabulary of any other language with its two million plus words.

However, English is anything but a precise language. Otherwise, why is it that when I wind up my watch I start it and when I wind up this chapter I end it? I look in vain for egg in eggplant, or for pine or an apple in a pineapple, or for a glimpse of ham in hamburger. How is it that a "slim chance" and a "fat chance" mean the same thing? How do you explain to a visitor from another country that your house "burns up" as it "burns down?" Why do we recite at a play and play at a recital? Why do we drive on a parkway and park in the driveway? If a vegetarian eats vegetables, what does a humanitarian eat? Should you care to explore more of these anomalies spend some time reading *Crazy English*, written in 1989 by Richard Lederer. [2]

This plot of confusion concerning the English language enlarges as you cross cultures. This explains why General Motors Corporation did not do well in their sales of the Chevrolet Nova model to the Spanish-speaking clientele. "No va" in Spanish means "no go." Who wanted to buy a car that would not go?

Who is there who hasn't laughed at Yogi Berra's use of malapropisms, especially when "cash is just as good as money?" Berra is also famous for his use of "weasel words," words whose meanings are difficult to "pin" down.

---

[1] Hayakawa, S. I., *Language in Thought and Action*, 4th ed.; Orlando, FL: Harcourt Brace Jovanovich, 1978.

[2] Lederer, Richard, *Crazy English*, published by Pocket Books, a division of Simon and Schuster of New York, NY, 1989.

Recall, too, his mispronunciations. Berra is a "folk hero" and by hero I do not mean a sandwich.

Since language varies so much in abstraction, in cultural contexts, and reality changes, and because meanings are deeply embedded within people, it becomes apparent that communication is not an easy process and the setting of measurement standards in communication, as elsewhere, is not always a "this is it!" Letter-high can be elusive. What say you?

THREE

CALLING AN AUDIBLE

Calling an audible is a football term that can be of immense value to anyone coping with change. Here's why.

Standard operating procedure for the quarterback is to call the next play in the huddle and send his team into formation to execute the play as designed and practiced many times. Every play has a number and once that number is called on the line the center snaps the ball and the team goes into action immediately.

Here's the hitch. If the quarterback approaches the line of scrimmage and sees the opposing team shift into a different defense that might easily cause the prearranged plan to fail, he calls an "audible." This tells his teammates that a change is in order. A new play that might succeed against this new defense must be tried. For instance, cancel the pass play to the tight end and go with a fullback rush between the left tackle and left guard with the right halfback doing the blocking. The old signal is "off" and a new signal indicates the change, often under stress since the time clock for that play is "running down" and a penalty might be assessed.

This is a short course in football strategy but it is a good analogy for coping with change. It relates to the obvious reality of change, the necessity for doing so, and what is often the pressure associated with dealing with change. Indirectly, it allows for the realization that the change may fail, cause a degree of confusion, and make matters even worse.

But change is a fact of life. Opportunities for change are staggering. David R. Gergen, Editor-at-Large for *U.S. News & World Report*, describes it this way, "Events have suddenly gone on fast forward so that we are whirling through history at a dizzying speed. Every dateline brings news of incredible changes."

The proliferation of changes in society has caused some people to be "shell-shocked" by the overwhelming amount of information they must accumulate to cope. To quote from an advertisement in a 1990 issue of the *Wall Street Journal* considering information overload, "The flood has arrived, may we interest you in an ark?"

Change itself is not unique. It's the proliferation and the profound revolutionary character of change that are unprecedented. Change can be extremely beneficial, but too rapid a change in any given area can produce a potent, even paralyzing negative effect. It's possible, because of threats emerging from its unpredictable qualities, that changes will cause some people to retreat and to resist change because of the fear of the unknown.

I recall seeing an Orange Pekoe tea bag that carried this message with it, "The best way to cope with change is to create it." In essence that is saying, "Don't leave change to chance; create it by choice."

The *initiation of change*, performed by change agents, is critical but the need does not stop there. There must be *change management* also. This is done by change managers. George Bernard Shaw was a change agent. He declared, "Some men see things as they are, and ask why; I dream of things that never were, and ask why not?"

Managing change requires people with skills in building bridges, in forming alliances, in dealing with stress, and in understanding values and priorities. It is true, also, when comprehending trends and philosophical differences, coping with cultural diversities and relational situations, and management expertise. There are numerous change managers but not all of them are extremely competent. Some react rather than pro-act. Strenuous concentration and bold action are required to plan new paradigms initiated by change agents.

It was H. H. Horne, a person who used to challenge John Dewey on numerous occasions at New York University, who acknowledged, "We frequently live our way into patterns of thinking rather than think our way into patterns of living."

Will there be failures while initiating and managing change? Of course! But remember, not the Alamo, but *Proverbs 24:16* which says, "For a righteous man falls seven times, and rises again." That's God's way of saying that a righteous person can fail many times but bounce back. Keep in mind that just as kites rise against, not with the wind, we will accomplish many great things through making changes when those changes are needed.

Back to the football analogy, remember that much strategic planning and experimentation went into the preparation to succeed on the football field. When the need for a change arose the wise team leader was ready for the occasion and "*called an audible.*" Let us follow the leader. Are you willing to do so? What say you?

FOUR

AS IF

This may come as a shock to those who "worship" at the shrine of science. Many principles of science are in fact hypothetical.

It was the German philosopher Hans Vaihinger (1852-1933) who coined the "As If Hypothesis" in 1911. He made it clear why he did this. His intention was to describe how thinking and acting proceeded by unproven or contradictory assumptions which were treated *as if* they were unquestionably true.

In his research, Vaihinger came to the conclusion that knowledge is a network of a series of "as if" strategies. To bring this hypothesis down to layman's language, he believed that when the thought processes formulate a coherent conjecture the tendency is to take this by faith and build upon it, to continue with further investigation on the assumption that it is probably true. The "as if hypothesis" developed into an *as if philosophy* which is a very real part of our everyday life.

It involves the intricate speculations about evolution, and even affects the "fact" that we pump gasoline into the tanks of our cars without scientifically checking to see if it really is gasoline rather than kerosene, diesel fuel or water. If the pump reads 92 octane how do we know if it isn't 87 octane unless we hear a pinging noise in the engines of our automobiles?

Underlying the *as if philosophy* is the principle of faith, the confidence to believe that it is true and reasonable.

Vaihinger's "as if hypothesis" emerged from the skeptical "*als ob* literary theory" that he espoused as early as 1876 when he was only 24 years of age. This theory attributed an idealistic attitude toward human motives for the sake of some desired goal. In the final analysis it meant the willingness to believe a lie if it would advance the cause.

Vaihinger may have borrowed some of his ideas from the English poet and critic, Samuel Taylor Coleridge (1772-1834). Coleridge expressed his ideas on the "willing suspension of disbelief" theory in 1815 when he wrote his *Literary Theory*. This theory cited the reader's agreement to accept without doubt the provisional truth of fiction in poetry by granting to "shadows of imagination" a temporary credulity. Thus, that "willing suspension of disbelief" for the moment constituted Coleridge's poetic faith.

The consistent pattern in the *as if philosophy* was referred to as faith which is an invitation for us to explore more closely what is meant by *faith*.

Before we take this "leap into faith" let us indicate, first of all, that the English word "science" comes from the Latin "scientia," meaning *knowledge*. In the Bible, both Old and New Testaments, science and knowledge translate the same Hebrew and Greek words respectively. The bottom line, then, is that science is what we know to be true; it is not naturalistic speculation. The Bible advocates truthful sciences and warns against false sciences, so called *(cf. First Timothy 6:20).*[1]

What is *faith*? Lloyd John Ogilvie writes, "True faith is not white-knuckled, teeth-gritting determination to survive in trouble."[2] Ogilvie is writing about the true faith. Charles Swindoll agrees. He said, "When it comes to faith, there is no substitute for the real things."[3]

---

[1] Unless otherwise indicated, Scripture quotations are taken from the *New American Standard Bible* (NASB), © 1960, 1977, 1995 by the Lockman Foundation. Other Scripture quotations, taken form other sources will be designated by name.

[2] Ogilvie, Lloyd J., *God's Best For My Life*, Eugene, Oregon: Harvest Home Publishers, p. 151.

[3] Swindoll, Charles, *Day By Day*. Nashville, TN: W Publishing Group, a Division of Thomas Nelson, Inc. 2000, p. 352.

John Bisagno informs his readers that "Faith is at the heart of life. You go to a doctor whose name you cannot pronounce, he gives you a prescription you cannot read, you take it to a pharmacist you don't know, he gives you medication you don't understand – and you take it. That's faith!"[4]

Is faith important? S. G. Holland, former Prime Minister of New Zealand, answers this inquiry with these words, "Faith draws the poison from every grief, takes the sting from every loss, and quenches the fire of every pain; and only faith can do it."[5] To that declaration of faith Abraham Heschel adds, "Faith like Job's cannot be shaken, because it is the result of having been shaken."[6]

John Maxwell gives an account of attending the funeral of Jane Chapman, wife of his good friend Tom Chapman. Maxwell said that during the funeral service a poem was read as follows: "I am standing on the seashore. A ship appears, spreads her white sails to the morning breeze and starts for the ocean. She is an object of beauty and I stand watching her till at last she fades away on the horizon. Somebody at my side says 'She is gone.' Gone where? Gone from my vision, that is all; she is just as large as when I saw her last. The diminished size and loss of sight is in me, not her; and just at the moment when someone at my side says, 'She is gone,' there are others who are watching her coming, and voices take up the joyful shout, 'Here she comes!'"[7] This is faith in action.

When people use *faith* to indicate what is possible but uncertain, that's not real faith. The ancient Hebrews used the word *'aman* to define faith which to them meant firmness and certainty. It affirms truth; it denies doubt. It offers safety; it discredits falseness. This Old Testament word spoke of certainty as a subjective conviction based upon the objective reality of God and His truth.

Trusting God is the heart and soul of the faith in the New Testament that centers upon the Lord Jesus Christ, and is best expressed in the whole range of meanings surrounding the Greek word, *pistis*, meaning faith. Knowing

---

[4] Bisagno, John, *The Word For You Today*, Roswell, GA: The Word For You Today Publisher, 2005, p. 9.
[5] *Ibid.*
[6] *Ibid.*
[7] *Ibid.*

15

and believing are linked. Likewise, life and faith are joined together. Death is associated with unbelief.

All of this occurs in contrast to belief in its purely natural exercise, an exercise which is expressed by W. E. Vine as that which "...consists of an opinion held in good faith without necessary reference to its proof."[8]

In other words, *real faith* – "the substance of things hoped for, the evidence of things not seen" *(Hebrews 11:1)* is not an "as if hypothesis." Real faith gives to us a genuine unchanging faith in a constantly changing world. And for this we should be grateful.

A few decades ago Dr. Francis Schaeffer pictured our culture as one that had its feet planted firmly in midair. Because of this genuine faith in God and His truth we can have our feet planted firmly on the ground. What could be better? It's no longer "as if" but "because of." What say you?

---

[8] Vine, W. E., *An Expository Dictionary of New Testament Words*. Old Tappan, New Jersey: Fleming H. Revell Company, 1966, p. 7.

FIVE

IF ONLY

Les Parrott III describes a scene in a busy newspaper office in which the editor shouts to one of his reporters, "There's a fire raging out of control west of town, and I want you to get there fast. And above all, get some good shots. If that means you have to hire an airplane, just do it. Don't worry about the expense."

Parrott continues, "The reporter, taking complete control of his assignment, called and ordered a plane. He rushed out to the airport, spotted a small aircraft with a young pilot in it, pulled open the door, jumped in, and ordered the pilot to take off. As directed, the pilot barreled down the runway and had just gotten the plane to a cruising altitude when the reporter said to him: 'See that fire raging to the west? I want you to fly over that and get as close to the fire as we can.'

'Incredulous,' the pilot replied, 'You want me to fly over that fire?'

'Absolutely,' the reporter said, 'I'm a photojournalist, and I need dramatic shots of that fire!'

The pilot glanced over with a quizzical look on his face and said, 'You mean you're not the flight instructor?'"[1]

---

[1] Parrott III, Les, *The Control Freak*. Wheaton, Illinois: Tyndale House Publishers, 2000, p. 153.

Take an educated guess. Do you think the scene would have been different *if only* both the pilot and the photojournalist had known the true facts?

If only Turkey had not closed the Dardanelles to Allied Forces ships in March of 1915, World War I might have ended much sooner with Germany's defeat. *If only* Italian master painter Constantino Brumidi had not stepped back on the scaffolding in the vast rotunda of the United States Capitol Building while painting the frieze in 1879, he would not have lost his balance and plunged downward. Even though Brumidi managed to grasp the sliding platform and hung on fifty-eight feet above the floor until rescuers came, the shock was too much for his heart and he died a few months later with his commissioned work half-done at the seventh panel.

If only Franz Schubert (1797-1828) would not have put down his pen while composing the Symphony No. 8 in B Minor before completing the task we would not have "the Unfinished Symphony."

If only Joshua, Moses' successor, would have defeated completely Israel's enemies as God instructed him to do in order to occupy the Promised Land the situation might be much different today.

If only Abraham and Sarah had been more patient in waiting for God to fulfill His promise to them concerning an heir would we know the conflicts that have followed through many centuries?

Recall the song mournfully sung by Tevye, the main character of *Fiddler On The Roof?* Over and over he repeated, "If I were a rich man…" As he sang he pondered his sad experiences in life. *If only* he was richer he thought he would be much happier.

If only Mstislav Rostropovich, the famous Russian musician, would have refused to risk his life and his career to give safe asylum to Alexander Solzhenitsyn we would not have the profound writings of Solzhenitsyn on Lenin and Stalin and the terrible tyranny that came to the Russian people after Nicholas II, the last Czar of Russia, was ruthlessly removed from power.

If only Gioacchino Rossini had not developed his overture to his six-hour opera, *William Tell,* with his galloping call of the trumpet there would not have been the famous signature tune that made the Lone Ranger known throughout the world.

If only Ira Sankey had kept quiet instead of singing in a muffled voice William Bradbury's hymn, "Savior, Like A Shepherd Lead Us," while standing guard duty one night in 1862 during the Civil War, he would have been shot by a Christian Confederate soldier whose rifle was aimed at Sankey's head. Instead, his life was spared that night at Sharpsburg, Maryland and Ira Sankey gave much to the ministry of music as song leader and hymn writer for Evangelist Dwight L. Moody for decades to follow.

As we know 1932 was one of the years of the Great Depression in our nation. It was also a time of physical and spiritual depression for musician Thomas A. Dorsey when he learned that his wife had died while delivering their child. He sorrowed deeply. While in the state of morning, Dorsey sat down at the piano and toyed with the keys. Slowly a tune emerged: "Precious Lord, take my hand, lead me on, let me stand, I am tired, I am weak, I am worn. Through the storm, through the night, lead me on to the light. Take my hand, precious Lord, lead me home." *If only* Thomas A. Dorsey had not written that song he would have never been considered the father of gospel music and that song unwritten and never played, would never have been thought of as one of the greatest gospel songs ever composed.

Your life and mine are full of "*if only's.*" They come packaged as projections of hope, based upon either realistic expectations or wishful thinking. Just as the nexus of the *"As if"* in the previous chapter found its source in *faith*, so "*If only*" has its roots in the expectations of *hope*.

Casual use of the word *hope* is often uttered in a wavering uncertain tone which ties in rather easily with the *"If only"* expression. It lacks the eager expectation of the "I look forward to" certainty that confident hope gives, a sense of what is desired will happen.

The Old Testament patriarch Job gives us an excellent example of the tentative hope when he cries out, "Where now is my hope? And who regards my hope?"[2]

---

[2] Job 17:15

Tentative hope often leads to "wishful thinking." We see this expressed in the comment of Job's so-called friend, Eliphaz, when he taunts Job with the message, "Is not your fear of God your confidence, and the integrity of you ways your hope?"[3]

For the most part, hope is the expectation of something, usually something we wait for patiently. The *Bible* tells us that hope is a purifying agent[4] that brings us great joy.[5] Since this hope is God-given it is steadfast and trustworthy. It changes the '*if only*' to '*since*.' And, it is available to everyone. What say you?

---

[3] Job 4:6
[4] First John 3:3
[5] Romans 12:12

SIX

INTERRUPTIONS

Attitude is important. Interruptions seem to be designed to test your attitudes.

If it is a test and the first question is in the completion category how would you answer: "I consider an interruption for the most part to be ...." Would your response be an intrusion, an invasion of privacy, a normal experience of life, a special challenge, a temporary "break," an interesting aside, an impolite thing to do, that which "ticks me off," or a stinging irritation?

Would it make a difference who did the interrupting? Would the social setting factor of just you and the interrupter differ from it happening when a crowd of others were witnessing the action?

Could the interruption lead to a serendipitous moment with its unexpected pleasure, to use a word coined by Horace Walpole? This happens frequently at birthday parties.

Is it possible that an interruption could transform a life? If it were possible to ask this question of the Apostle Paul as he traveled on the road to Damascus *(Acts 9:1-16)*, what might he say? Or, if the same were true and we could inquire of the woman at the well whom Jesus interrupted *(John 4:7-29)*,[1] what might her answer be?

---

[1] The Bible verses referenced in this chapter are taken from *The New Scofield Reference Bible*, New York: Oxford University Press, 1967.

J. B. Phillips may have had unwelcome interruptions in mind, among other things, when he wrote his paraphrase of *James 1:2-4* – "When all kinds of trials and temptations crowd into your lives, my brothers, don't resent them as intruders, but welcome them as friends! Realize that they come to test your faith and to produce in you the quality of endurance. But let the process go on until that endurance is fully developed, and you will find you have become men of mature character with the right sort of independence. And if, in the process, any of you does not know how to meet any particular problem he has only to ask God – who gives generously to all men without making them feel foolish or guilty – and he may be quite sure that the necessary wisdom will be given him."[2]

I started this chapter by saying that attitude is important. An *attitude* is a relatively stable learned emotional predisposition to respond in a consistent manner toward persons, objects, or situations. An attitude is either a positive or a negative feeling that affects our perceptions and influences our overt behavior.

This definitive characteristic can best be demonstrated by the Apostle Paul's description of the two most important qualities of love presented in *First Corinthians 13:4*. Those attributes are *patience* and *kindness*. Patience is the inner attitude and kindness is the outer action. When that combination goes to work a person becomes a release person of God's love who gives to others what they *need*, not what he or she thinks they *deserve*.

Let me put this into perspective. Bob Considine, writing for *The Boston Globe*, gave an account of the story of Carl and Edith Taylor of Waltham, Massachusetts. This married couple was living on a very limited income and found it difficult to pay their monthly bills even though both worked and they had no children. Discouraged with this situation, Carl decided to accept an offer to go to Okinawa where he could earn more money. He would go alone and send for Edith later. Edith was to keep her job and remain in Waltham in the meantime.

Once separated they both wrote daily to each other. Each looked forward to the other's correspondence and longed for their reunion. The months went by with Carl sending much of his overseas income home to

---

[2] Phillips, J. B., *The New Testament in Modern English*. London: Geoffrey Bles, 1960, p. 478.

Edith. As the months added up to a couple of years with still no reuniting, Carl's letters became less frequent although Edith wrote everyday. Finally, Carl's letters ceased altogether and no money was sent to Edith to help her defray the expenses at home.

Then the bombshell exploded. Carl wrote to Edith and said that he had secured a divorce in Okinawa and had married a Japanese woman by the name of Iko. Edith was stunned and devastated and cried for days from the emotional pain. Several years passed before an unexpected letter came from Carl addressed to Edith.

In his letter Carl explained that he was expected to die soon from terminal cancer. Iko would have very little money to live on and he asked Edith if she would be willing to let their two young daughters, Maria and Helen, come to the States to live with Edith. What a strange request from someone who had broken his marriage vows, perhaps illegally, and married another woman under such unusual circumstances.

Once the shock wore off and the renewed hurt was resolved, Edith decided that she would honor Carl's request and invite the young girls to come to Massachusetts. Before she wrote her letter back to Carl she took time to pray about it and to give it further thought. Edith decided to expand the invitation to include the destitute Iko, the woman who had taken her place as Carl's wife. She sent the invitation and included some money to help with their travel expenses. By that time Carl had died.

The day arrived when the plane from Okinawa landed at Logan airport in Boston. Edith was exceptionally nervous as she awaited their stepping off the ramp from the airplane. Could she understand their language or accent? What would their relationship be like?

After all the other passengers had come off the plane, following a pause, a short oriental lady, somewhat stooped over got off the ramp with two young girls beside her. They were headed toward customs when Edith Taylor caught up to them. Edith embraced Iko and then hugged Maria and Helen. Tears streamed down Edith's face.

Bob Considine ended his article by asking the question, "What would you have done if you had been in Edith's position?"

What Edith did was to show much love through patience and kindness following the greatest interruption in her life. Interruptions test our attitudes. Let's make sure we pass the test for godliness when they occur. What say you?

SEVEN

ASSUMPTIONS

Crawford W. Loritts is a servant of God that I respect greatly, as do many others. He began his ministerial voyage in life as a missionary in the inner-city of Philadelphia. He was with the American Missionary Fellowship, America's oldest home mission agency with roots dating back to 1790. Crawford left the mission to move on to other challenges just a short time before I became the General Director of AMF. I have followed his career carefully.

Dr. Loritts eventually became the national director of the Church Resource Group of Campus Crusade for Christ. The late Bill Bright, Founder and President of Campus Crusade for Christ International, called Crawford his beloved friend and co-laborer and admired his passionate commitment to Christ, his effective leadership and his ability to communicate the Gospel to many thousands he addressed in numerous conferences, conventions, churches, colleges and universities throughout the world.

Recently, Dr. Loritts and his wife Karen, who is his partner in life and ministry, accepted a call to become the senior minister of a large church in Roswell, Georgia, a suburb of Atlanta. Crawford W. Loritts authored a book in 1989 which was entitled *A Passionate Commitment* which challenges people, especially Christians, to recapture their sense of purpose in life. In his book, Dr. Loritts has this to say about the subject of *assumptions*.

A few years ago my wife Karen and I were invited to a friend's house for dinner. We had been in their home before and I was familiar with the area, so I thought there would be no problem finding the house. Wrong! We drove around for more than an hour, frustrated because we knew we were only a few blocks away, but we couldn't find the place. Not only were we lost, but I also had to deal with Karen's I-told-you-so's. This experience is a reminder that assumptions can get you into trouble. A quick phone call before we left the house would have saved us from all that hassle and stress.[1]

Assumptions have gotten many Christians into spiritual hot water. Jesus Christ came to give us an abundant, fruitful Christianity, filled with specific direction and purpose. Although we have a general sense of direction, many of us have assumed that either somehow we can work out the details, or somehow everything will fall into place. We fail to realize that we do not live in a favorable or even neutral environment. Everyday our commitment to Christ is assaulted by the world, the flesh and the devil. Therefore, our Christianity must take the *offensive*. It must be *intentional*.

The word *assume*, among other meanings assigned to it, has the primary meaning of taking too much for granted. It is the action of being presumptuous or suppositional. It implies putting on a false appearance, although it may be with a harmless or excusable motive.

The question we ask ourselves is not whether we have ever done that. We not only assume but we know we have. The question is how often do we do it and with what consequences. *Assumptions* not only lead to rationalizations as an attempt to justify our actions, but they lead to unrealistic expectations and frustrating relationships.

Dr. Loritts indicates clearly that to help with this problem we must take the offensive, be proactive in an intentional manner. What say you?

2 Loritts, Crawford W., *A Passionate Commitment*. San Bernardino, CA: Here's Life Publishers, Inc. 1989, p. 15.

EIGHT

UNDER THE RADAR

Paul Revere was a pre-radar personality. Had radar been available to him on that memorable night of April 18, 1775, he might have been able to detect British troop movements with greater precision and would not have relied on a general cry of alarm, "The British are coming!" as he galloped on his horse through the Massachusetts countryside trying to reach every Middlesex village en route.

Revere's famous ride was in 1775. It wasn't until 1842 that Christopher Andreas Doppler, an Austrian physicist, observed that the frequency of light and sound waves were affected by the "relative motion of the source and the detector." Later, in 1887, a German physicist named Heinrich Hertz began experimenting with electromagnetic radio waves in his laboratory. He detected and measured radio frequencies in oscillations per second. His laboratory discoveries led to the invention of both radio and radar.

However, it took the work of the Scottish physicist, Sir Robert Alexander Watson-Watt (1892-1973) to perfect the discoveries of Doppler and Hertz so that radar could be used to locate flying aircraft. He got a British patent for radar in April of 1935. Dr. Robert Rines, the inventor of the high definition radar and the sonogram, and Luis Walter Alvarez, who invented a radio distance and direction indicator and a landing system for aircrafts, and a radar system for locating planes, added quality components to the scientific radar development.

My life was impacted by the work these men did and by the accomplishments they achieved. Briefly let me tell you how this is.

Toward the end of World War II, and near the beginning of 1945, I was flying a C-47 as first pilot for the United States Air Force in the European Theatre of Operations. By that time I had over 320 hours of actual combat flying time with the 76th Squadron of the 435th Troop Carrier Group carrying paratroopers of the 82nd and 101st Airborne groups behind enemy lines, towing gliders into enemy territories, picking up severely wounded soldiers on the front lines and transporting them back to base hospitals. Another part of our missions was to take much needed and critical supplies to such armies as those commanded by Generals George C. Patton and Courtney H. Hodges, 3rd and 1st armies respectively.

On a day I shall long remember, I was flying right wing in a three-plane formation led by our squadron commander. The weather was inclement with ice and snow gathering on the leading edge of our wings faster than the "boots" could shake them off. We were flying dangerously close to the treetops in order to avoid radar detection by the Germans. Each of our three planes was transporting over one hundred jerry cans of gasoline for Hodges' tanks, considerable ammunition, medical supplies, and food for our soldiers in the front lines.

As we crossed the Rhine river between Cologne and Ramagen at an altitude of 300 feet, we encountered intense flak from a German anti-aircraft unit. My plane was closest to the source of the firepower. In a flashing moment of time, both engines were hit and on fire. Then the cabin containing the gasoline, ammunition and other supplies took a direct hit and was in flames. Since it takes a minimum of 400 feet of altitude to bail out safely, it was necessary to crash land this burning inferno as soon as possible before we all were cremated alive.

In an area, the only stretch at that time along the Rhine river for nine miles that wasn't lined by trees, I crash landed the burning C-47 in a rhubarb patch. The other members of the crew and I evacuated the plane immediately, just seconds before it blew up in a terrible explosion sending flames and billows of smoke high into the air. God had wonderfully spared our lives even though we were to become "guests" of the Germans in Stalag Luft 6-G for the remaining day for the war in Germany.

As long as we flew "off the deck" just above the treetops we escaped radar detection. We were *under the radar.* The moment we were exposed crossing the Rhine at 300 feet by the radar we became easy targets for their massive fire power.

There's an analogous lesson here that applies to each of us. When we sin and do wrong things, as long as we feel safe from detection, we are apt to keep on doing that which we should not do. Some people *fly under the radar* for long periods of time thinking that all is well since they feel no one knows about it and they go unpunished. Then, when "society's radar" exposes us we feel ashamed, guilty, and vulnerable to punishment. All along God's radar has exposed our motives as well as our actions.

It may be a policeman's radar gun that catches us. We are "caught" and must pay the fine. In the financial world, a person guilty of fraud may not be exposed for years but when he or she is, it means conviction and jail time. The pedophile may prey on small children with seeming impunity but the day of detection comes and the price of punishment is high. The list of examples could go on *ad infinitum* and *ad nauseum.* Like out plane, being "under the radar" appeared to give us safe haven. Once exposed, the danger was imminent. Obviously, the high cost of a low life becomes evident.

But the sad story doesn't end there. There is *never* a time when you are "under the radar" in God's eyes. The writer of *Proverbs 15:3* states: "The eyes of the Lord are in every place, watching the evil and the good." God is omniscient (knows everything) and omnipresent (is everywhere at the same time).

Moreover, *Proverbs 5:21* reveals, "For the ways of man are before the eyes of the Lord, and He watches all his paths." God closely watches us and weighs all that we do. He knows the thoughts and the intents of the heart. In *Hebrews 4:12* we have this confirmed that God is "...able to judge the thoughts and the intentions of the heart." Even before we sin against Him and others, God is fully aware of what is taking place.

But the story doesn't stop there either. There is the punishment phase of un-confessed and un-forgiven sin and it is *fatal*. Here is the verdict in *Romans 6:23* – "For the wages of sin is death…" I'm thrilled that that verse of Scripture doesn't stop there. It goes on to read: "…but the free gift of God is eternal life in Christ Jesus our Lord."

In summary, sinning against God is a universal malady. In God's eyes we are never "beneath the radar screen." God, through the sacrifice of His Son, has given us a way to escape the consequences of eternal death. He will forgive us and give to us eternal life if we heed the message of *Romans 10:9* and *10* – "That if you confess with your mouth Jesus as Lord, and believe in you heart that God raised Him from the dead, you shall be saved; for with the heart a man believes, resulting in righteousness, and with the mouth he confesses, resulting in salvation."

I'm glad that He did this! What say you?

NINE

MORAL COMPASS

The compass was a very important and much needed invention for navigation. Prior to its invention seafarers depended on the sun solely for navigational purposes, a difficult task during overcast days.

The Chinese invented the compass in the fourth century B.C. It was a simple piece of lodestone floating on water. Later, flat pieces of iron replaced the lodestone. In the sixth century A.D. a needle was introduced to this instrument.

By the latter half of the thirteenth century A.D. the English mounted a needle on a pin which became the foundational piece for what later became the highly sophisticated compass in use today for simple purposes worldwide, especially for navigational aids on ships and airplanes.

Just as the compass as a navigational instrument has developed over the centuries, so has the definition of what is meant by a compass expanded to meet society's needs. Almost any modern dictionary, for example, will define a compass as that which goes around completely giving a full extent of range It will say that a compass is any of various instruments, consisting of a magnetic needle that swings freely on a pivot and points to the magnetic north for showing direction. Among other descriptions, it claims that a compass is that which helps to grasp mentally, to comprehend fully, to understand realistically.[1]

---

[1] Webster's *New World Dictionary of the American Language*, Second College Edition. New York: Simon & Schuster, 1970, p. 289.

It is this last definition that has a direct bearing on what happened to a bright, overly-ambitious man by the name of Jeb Stuart Magruder. As the flyleaf of his autobiography, *An American Life, One Man's Road to Watergate*, states: "For the first thirty–seven years of his life, Jeb Stuart Magruder lived the American dream. A charming, intelligent, intensely ambitious young man, he worked his way through college, married the right girl, fathered four handsome children, and all the while worked his way up the corporate and political ladders at a dizzying pace, until in 1969 he was called to Washington to serve as a Special Assistant to President Nixon. He loved the power and excitement of the White House, and it seemed that a life of limitless success awaited him."[2]

In 1972, Magruder's dream turned into a nightmare. He wasn't alone as the Watergate burglary exposed the complicity of others in this bungled attempt to burglarize the offices of the Democratic political party. Among them were such personalities as James McCord, G. Gordon Liddy, H. R. (Bob) Halderman, E. Howard Hunt, John W. Dean, Charles Colson, John Ehrlichman, John Mitchell, and others including President Richard Nixon.

When the dust finally settled, Jeb Stuart Magruder stood before Judge John J. Sirica to await the pronouncement of his jail sentence on a charge of perjury. The Judge asked Magruder if he had anything to say. Mr. Magruder made a remark at that moment that has been etched in stone in the memories of many persons since. His response to Judge Sircia, in essence was this, "Somewhere along the line I wanted to win so badly that I lost my moral compass."

This brilliant young man, a graduate of Williams College in the Berkshire Mountains in northwestern Massachusetts and the husband of the former Gail Nicholas, was labeled a "Watergate crook," by NBC News commentator David Brinkley and sentenced to jail by Judge John J. Sircia. By his own admission, Jeb Magruder confessed, "Obviously, in my case, ambitions led to disaster."[3]

---

[2] Magruder, Jeb Stuart, *An American Life, One Man's Road to Watergate*. New York: Athenaeum, 1974, Inside Front Cover.

[3] *Ibid.*, p. 316.

Strong ambitions are to be commended if one keeps his balance and his moral compass pointing in the right direction. The choices are ours to make and our destiny is determined by those choices. What say you?

TEN

QUANTUM THINKING

Quantum thinking challenges assumptions. It breaks habits. It changes mental models and rearranges cognition. It often works "outside the box" of the realms of logical thought and reasoned structures. It triggers insight.

The opposite of *quantum thinking* is to think within a narrow and inflexible spectrum, a spectrum that is reinforced especially by tradition and educational institutions. Its world view is mechanistic and limited in scope.

Quantum thinking is a constant series of appeals to God knowing that He knows. It's like a certain youthful Joyce who prayed: "Dear God, Thank you for the baby brother, but what I asked for was a puppy. I never asked for anything before. You can look it up."[1]

To the ancient Romans *quantus* referred to "how much." This is why a *quantum leap* concerns any sudden and extensive change or advance regarding any significant issue. Dr. Ravi Zacharias, one of my students at the seminary where I served as a professor, is a quantum thinker *par excellent.*

In his book, *Deliver Us From Evil,*[2] Zacharias proves with great insight and clarity of thought how so many of the popular ideas of today are vandalizing our abilities to think and to act. This dynamic person and brilliant thinker shows how secularization has led to a loss of shame, pluralization to a loss of reason, and privitization to a loss of meaning. What he says is explosive

---

[1] *The Saturday Evening Post*, July/August. 2005 Edition, p. 18.
[2] Zacharias, Ravi. *Deliver Us From Evil*, Dallas: Word Publishing, 1996.

and quantum thinking with convincing passion that opens our minds to the grandeur and grace of God.

Not for a moment would I minimize the amazing insights given to the world by German theoretical physicist Max Karl Ernst Plank (1858-1947), winner of the 1918 Nobel prize for physics, for his work on thermodynamics and black-body radiation which caused him to set aside classical dynamical principles and to develop the *quantum theory*.[3] Obviously, he was a quantum thinker. However, the greatest of all quantum thinkers is God who has the power and the ability to do things that are "exceeding abundantly beyond all that we ask or think."[4]

It was the Old Testament prophet Isaiah who points out the fact that God Himself revealed to Israel and to the world that His thoughts "are not your thoughts, neither are your ways His ways."[5] To that, Isaiah added the quantum acknowledgement that God said: "For as the heavens are higher than the earth, so are My ways higher than your ways, and My thoughts than your thoughts."[6]

The Apostle Paul of the New Testament caught the spirit of God's quantum thinking ability when he exclaimed to the Roman Christians: "Oh the depth of the riches both of the wisdom and knowledge of God! How unsearchable are His judgments and unfathomable Hs ways! For who has known the mind of the Lord, or who became His counselor?"[7]

There is an avenue of access to gain some of God's wisdom and it comes to those who by faith trust in God for eternal salvation through two tremendous provisions He has made. One is the inward presence of the Holy Spirit, very God Himself. As the Apostle Paul writes in First Corinthians,[8] the Holy Spirit searches the deep things of God and makes them available to those who trust God by revealing them through the Bible, which is God's second provision. God the Holy Spirit compares spiritual things with Spirit-taught

---

[3] Bothamley, Jennifer, *Dictionary of Theories*. London: Gale Research International Ltd., 1993, p 414.

[4] *New Testament*, Ephesians 3:20.

[5] *Old Testament*, Isaiah 55:8.

[6] *Ibid.* Isaiah 55:9.

[7] *New Testament*, Romans 11:33,34.

[8] *Ibid.*, First Corinthians 2:10-13.

36

words. This is a foretaste of knowing the quantum thinking of God for the purpose-driven life that Rick Warren refers to in his books.

Do you remember the humorous and incongruous comment of Yogi Berra on a television commercial when he says with a straight face, "And they give you cash, which is just as good as money?" This is an interesting aside relating to the value assessment. For example, when you purchase an awning are you really buying welcome shade. Max Anders deals with this subject when he writes, "We don't buy glasses; we buy vision…we don't buy a newspaper; we buy information."[9] But the *quantum thinking* occurs when Anders makes the profound comment, "God wants us to have wealth. We must be careful not to settle for money."[10] The vast wealth of God's Word is intended to stretch our finite minds into areas of thinking that can only be attained with the guidance and power of the Holy Spirit of God.

The Apostle Paul, who encourages us to have the inner disposition of Jesus Christ,[11] urges us to consider "…whatever is true, whatever is honorable, whatever is right, whatever is pure, whatever is of good repute, if there is any excellence and if anything worthy of praise, let your mind dwell on these things."[12]

We enter into *quantum thinking* spiritually speaking when we are filled with the knowledge of God's will in all wisdom and spiritual understanding.[13] This part of Paul's prayer ought to be our daily petition based on God's promises. What say you?

---

[9] Anders, Max, *The Good Life*. Dallas: Word Publishing, 1993, p.11.
[10] *Ibid.*, p.15.
[11] *New Testament*, Philippians 2:5.
[12] *Ibid.*, Philippians 4:8.
[13] *Ibid.*, Colossians 1:9.

ELEVEN

COUCH POTATO

Rather than an alternative to French Fries, a *couch potato* is suspended animation in the form of a personality who sits, and sits, and sits, or, if that is too much effort, simply reclines. The *couch potato* suffers from severe lethargy, a contagious condition for lazy people that leads to hardening of the arteries (streets and avenues) due to poor circulation among people. Horizontal inertia has trumped vertical action!

Couch potato is a slang expression in the English language that has made many English potato growers very angry. They would prefer that we substitute this term with something else, such as "chaise laze, or davenport dreary, or sofa spud, or lounger lazy, or couch slouch."

There is some doubt associated with the origin of the expression *couch potato*. It is believed that it first emerged in 1979 in order to give flair to those who relax in a mindless and slothful manner. If the British farmers are offended how is it that couch manufacturers are not offended also?

The French word *couche* means "a bed." It comes from the French verb *coucher* meaning "to lie down," which is most appealing to true *couch potatoes* who spend too much time in front of the television screen while eating fast foods and becoming increasingly obese.

When I hear the term *couch potato* being used it brings to mind the words of the song composed by Johnny Mercer and Hoagy Carmichael, and sung extremely well by the Supremes. It was entitled, "Lazy Bones."[1]

This catchy tune was matched by the intriguing lyrics:

> Lazy Bones, sleeping, sleeping in a noonday sun,
> Tell me, how you 'spect to get your days work done—
> Day's work done; you'll never get your day's work done,
> Sleeping, lazy bones, sleeping in a noonday sun.
>
> When days' dusk means praying,
> I bet you keep praying that all the bugs fall off the vine;
> And when you go fishing, I bet you keep wishing
> That the fish would never, never grab your line,
> You old lazy bones.
> Loafin', loafin, all through the day
> Tell me how you 'spect to make a dime that way,
> Dime that way, you'll never make a dime that way;
> Well look at him, lazy bones, never hear a word I say, lazy bones.

Now for a more serious look at what is involved in "couch potatoism," another expression for "lazyholics" which is definitely related to work ethics, or the lack of them.

If being lazy from time to time is a part of a temporary rest, it is perfectly acceptable and usually much needed to relax the mind and the body. If, on the other hand, laziness is a pattern of life it is offensive to God and destructive to the lives of others, especially those closest to us.

The Bible has much to say about laziness or slothfulness. Just the book of *Proverbs* alone reminds us of such admonitions as: "...diligent hands will rule, but laziness ends in slave labor *(Proverbs 12:24, NIV);*" "...all hard work brings a profit, but mere talk leads to poverty *(Proverbs 14:24, NIV);*" "One who is slack is brother to one who destroys *(Proverbs 18:9, NIV).*"[2]

The Apostle Paul stated forcefully in *Second Thessalonians 3:10, (NIV),* *"If a man will not work, he shall not eat."* The couch potato delights in not working but eating much in defiance of instruction of Scripture. Chronic

---

[1] From the Album: The Supremes Sing Country, Western & Pop Lyrics.
[2] *The New International Version (NIV),* Copyright © 1977, 1978, 1984, International Bible Society.

laziness from a biblical viewpoint is a sin. It violates God's standard of stewardship and should be overcome by obedience to God's Word and a decisive change in lifestyle. What say you?

TWELVE

CATCH – 22

"The heat of the dispute between Left and Right has grown so fierce in the last decade that the habits of civilized discourse have suffered a scorching," so wrote Saul Bellow in the forward of Allan Bloom's provocative book, *The Closing of the American Mind*.[1] That insightful comment was written in 1987 when the political dispute was in its earlier stages. Today, the "scorching" is a raging inferno between the Democrats and Republicans, seemingly out-of-control and with no end in sight.

As a consequence, Aristotle's three persuasive proofs of *ethos* (source credibility), *logos* (logical thinking), and *pathos* (emotional issues) have been reduced to *pathos* in its lowest common denominator.

Put this "argument jigsaw puzzle" together and you get a *catch-22*. The phrase *catch-22* comes from a satirical anti-war novel written by Joseph Heller in 1961.[2] Just the mention of Heller's name conjures up many seeming coincidences. An explanation is necessary.

Both Joseph Heller and I were born in the same year, 1923, and in the same state, New York, although he was born in Brooklyn and I in Corning. We both served in the United States Army Air Force. Heller was a bombardier in a B-25 who flew 60 combat missions. I was a pilot in a C-47 who had over 320 hours of combat flying. We both studied at Oxford, England. Heller

---

[1] Bloom, Allan, *The Closing of the American Mind*. New York: Simon & Schuster, 1987, p. 18.
[2] Heller, Joseph, *Catch-22*. New York: Scribner Paperback Fiction, Simon & Schuster, 1961.

was a Fulbright scholar at Oxford in 1949-50. I audited classes taught by C.S. Lewis at Magdalen College in 1944-45. We both taught on the faculty at Pennsylvania State University in the early 1950's. Even though I disagree sharply with some of Heller's views on certain subjects, I have used the term "Catch-22" many times over the years since Heller coined this phrase in 1961.

Catch-22 refers to a paradox in a law, a regulation, or a practice that is illogical and makes one a victim of its provision no matter what attempts are made to change the situation. It leads to a frustrating and confusing condition in which one is trapped by contradictory components. It is a dilemma that requires more than a little "catching-up" to overcome, if it is possible to do so which is unlikely. Actually, it is thought of as a "no-win" situation.

Ancient Job, patriarch and classic sufferer of Old Testament times, felt that way as he was exposed to great pain and mental anguish, and could not understand why all these catastrophes were happening to him. With unspeakable and unexpected suddenness everything that was solid and secure in his life came unglued and he had not one clue as to why. He lost his entire family through deaths, his entire wealth through circumstances, and he suffered immeasurable pain through sickness that seemed incurable. His running sores, satanically inspired, made him an outcast in society. His wife, before her untimely death, urged Job to "Curse God, and die!"[3] His three friends, Eliphaz, Bildad, and Zopher taunted him and tried their best to lay a "guilt trip" on him for sins he never committed. Job was in a *catch-22*.

To compound his agony Job did not have the needed advantage of a modern pain management clinic such as Mayo Clinic or John Hopkins Hospital could provide. He hurt deeply from a "total systems failure." It was not his autoimmune system, nor his cardio-vascular system that plagued him. It was his emotional-support system as his so called friends further messed-up his life with their pious pronouncements and "traditional insights," that would have pleased someone like Tevye, the main character in *The Fiddler On The Roof*, a "traditional victim." Small wonder, that in a moment of great weakness, Job felt that God was unfair to him.

---

[3] *Old Testament*, Job 2:9.

Fortunately for Job the story did not end there. He finally emerged from his *catch-22* dilemma. He was healed by God. His faith in God got a booster-shot and his normal life was restored. In fact, in *Job 42:12*, Job admits that the Lord blessed him more in the latter end of his life than in the beginning.[4]

There was another Old Testament character whose life got caught up in a *catch-22* also. His name was Asaph and his story is told in *Psalm 73*. Job's problem was "Why do the righteous suffer?" With Asaph, it was "Why do the wicked prosper?"

Asaph was an outstanding singer, instrumentalist, and choir director with a super-sensitive spirit. He was so good as a musician that both David and Solomon, kings of Israel, chose him to be their chief musician. He also was a writer, given credit for developing twelve of the *Psalms* (50, 73-83). But Asaph has a serious *catch-22*. He was both agitated and anguished at the constant prosperity of the wicked individuals whose insolence and caustic skepticism defied God and destroyed the sensibilities of his friends and himself with their arrogant blasphemies. He both hated and envied them. He felt pain, perplexity, pressure, and was plagued continuously.[5] He was in a *catch-22* of super proportions. He confessed, "But as for me, my feet came close to stumbling; my steps had almost slipped."[6]

It took God's power, presence, and purposes to bring both Job and Asaph out of their respective *catch-22's*. We can learn a great deal from their experiences. Both men were provoked by their circumstances into saying many rash and illogical things. This is a warning to us. Both Job and Asaph had defective understandings of God's permissive will for their lives. They thought God had abandoned them, this same God Who is the same yesterday, today and forever,[7] and Who had promised that He will never, never let anyone go, or fail them, and Who will never, never give anyone up, abandon or desert them.[8]

---

[4] *Ibid.*, Job 42:12.

[5] *Ibid.*, Psalm 73:13-16.

[6] *Ibid.*, Psalm 73:2.

[7] *New Testament*, Hebrews 13:8.

[8] *Ibid.*, Hebrews 13:5 and 6.

We say never throw in the towel, even when faced with circumstances that seem utterly impossible. We say never give up, never throw up your hands in despair when confronted by *catch-22's*. We say, discover the unlimited resources of God and become release persons of God's power. What say you?

THIRTEEN

ROCK FORMATIONS

Mention *rock* and almost everyone in today's society thinks in terms of a form of music that embraces many different sounds with a hurried beat. As did *jazz, rock music* dates its origins to the *blues*.

Once Muddy Waters and Howlin' Wolf plugged in their electric guitars the pitch elevated and the volume intensified creating a harsh, loud sound. Disc jockey Alan Freed from Cleveland became enamored with this new form of music and coined the phrase "rock 'n roll."

Rock 'n roll's energetic beat and outlandish expressions of sexuality caught on quickly and large, sometimes raucous, crowds gathered to shout at their favorite musician with feverish enthusiasm. The rhythm and blues of the Afro-American musical tradition combined with country and western style music and produced the "King of Rock" Elvis Presley, rock music's first superstar. *Heartbreak Hotel* climbed to the top of the musical charts and Presley, who blended the rich tones and melodic country-and-western sound with the bouncy rhythms of rock 'n roll, turned his audiences into teenage frenzies as he added his pelvis-rolling, lip-pursing antics to his lyrics. The insatiable influence of affluent adolescents turned rock 'n roll into a multi-million dollar enterprise.

When the "fab four" of John Lennon, Paul McCartney, George Harrison, and Ringo Starr, all sons of working class families in Liverpool, England, got together to form the Beatles in 1962, international rock 'n roll music exploded. A new word, "Beatlemania," was coined to describe this phenomenon. The Beatles took this music form to a new height using the influence of gospel music, Baroque counterpoint, India's "raga" arrangements, country and western in their experimental compositions.

At a time when the Beatles were cutting back on their public appearances for more studio presentations along came another British group called The Rolling Stones, which made the Beatles look like altar boys. They wore shaggy-hair and used gypsy-like mannerisms. Mick Jaggar's singing was raspy, rude, and foul-mouthed. The initial hint of protest developed into a landslide. The Rolling Stones are more popular today than when they first hit the big-time.

And then there was Bob Dylan who gave birth to the "electric band." *Acid rock* was characterized by its mysterious, dream-like lyrics at a time when LSD and marijuana were being introduced to larger audiences. Eric Clapton and The Who created the "heavy noise" sound in rock 'n roll. The rhythm section of the band became more noticeable as The Temptations sang "My Girl." It took Ray Charles to bring prominent respect to the jazz-rock scene, even though his music is hard to classify. So much for rock music!

To the geologist, *rock* has an altogether different meaning. The geologist is involved in the scientific study of the development and structure of the earth's crust with various rock types.

The geologist not only knows that eight elements (oxygen, silicon, aluminum, iron, calcium, sodium, potassium, and magnesium) make up more than 98 percent of all the rocks in the world, but they also spend most of their time dealing with the three main kinds of rocks, which are *igneous, sedimentary,* and *metamorphic.*

Geologists concern themselves with the study of metamorphosed sedimentary rocks, lava flows, granite, limestone deposits, pumice, crystalline rocks, and various forms of mineral matter. Fossil rocks give an impression or trace of life that has been preserved in the rock, such as Petosky stones found in the northern part of the Lower Peninsula of the state of Michigan. Igneous rock is formed by the cooling of magma or lava. Sedimentary rock is formed by cementation of sediment such as sand, silt, mud or clay, or from plant and animal remains. A naturally-occurring substance with a particular composition and structure is mineral rock. Metamorphic rock emerges from the process of a rock changing due to extreme heat and pressure which, in turn, creates a new rock.

If we are not geologists, or if we do not study and collect rocks, our knowledge of this subject may be limited to knowing about the Rock of Gibraltar, a huge block of limestone, or about granite, an igneous rock that contains quartz, feldspar, and mica, seen in many places in cemeteries.

Geologic history of rocks can be a fascinating study and, indeed, it attracts numerous students in the universities of the world. However, there is a third "rock formation" that I would like to introduce.

The third reference, and to the Christian community the most important *rock formation* concerns God Himself. The Bible refers to the rocks beneath the shallow soil,[1] to rocky places,[2] and to "rough places"[3] where the translation relates to rocky ground. However, the primary reference is a figurative and metaphorical designation of Jesus Christ in such scriptural passages as *Romans 9:33; First Corinthians 10:4; Matthew 16:18; and First Peter 2:8.*

The Bible also speaks literally of rocks frequently, and is rich in metaphors which follow from Moses' first reference to God as a Rock in *Deuteronomy 32:4.* In the symbolism of the Bible, God is the Rock of His people, the Rock of Ages.

In the Hebrew language the word *tsur* referenced "a craggy height," and the word *sela* meant a mass of stone such as a mountain that served as a natural fortress.[4] The Greek language equivalent was the word *petra*, used both literally and figuratively.[5]

Such biblical verses as *Second Samuel 22:2; Psalm 18:2 and 71:3; and First Peter 2:8* link the word *rock* directly to God. When this occurs it is done to show the strength, reliability and safety of God's character and functioning abilities.

---

[1] *New Testament*, Matthew 13:5, 20.

[2] *Ibid.*, Mark 4:5.

[3] *Ibid.*, Acts 27:29.

[4] *Old Testament*, Exodus 17:6; Numbers 20:8; Judges 20:45, 47; First Samuel 23:25.

[5] *New Testament*, Matthew 7:24, 25; Mark 15:46; Matthew 16:18; First Peter 2:5.

Mountains point to the Creator God. Hannah confirmed this when she prayed, "Nor is there any rock *(sur) like our God"* (*First Samuel 2:2;* italics mine). The Psalmist affirmed the same as he sang, "My soul waits in silence for God only; from Him is my salvation. He only is my rock and my salvation, my stronghold; I shall not be greatly shaken…He only is my rock and my salvation, my stronghold; I shall not be shaken" *(Psalm 62:1, 2 and 6).* In this same Psalm, he adds, "Oh God my salvation and my glory rest; the rock of my strength, my refuge is in God."

What a remarkable difference between the music of rock 'n roll and that of the Psalmist whose rock was God. It was the difference of the secular sounds of syncopating serenaders and the sacred sentiments of worshiping servants of the most high God. What say you?

FOURTEEN

BALANCE

Under the definition of *symmetry*, *Webster's Dictionary* offers this succinct description of the word *balance*. *Balance* suggests "the offsetting or contrasting of parts so as to produce an aesthetic equilibrium in the whole."[1]

It was bodily equilibrium in particular that concerned the Flying Wallendas on that fateful day an indoor circus was being held in Detroit's Cobo Hall. The Wallenda family was in the process of building their incredible human pyramid on three levels of wire with no safety net beneath them. Four men were on the first level, three men on level two, and a woman balanced on a chair on the third or top level. They had performed this amazing feat before but on this fateful day something unexpected happened.

Dieter Wallenda, one of the first level men, suddenly felt his right knee begin to quiver. He cried out in the German language, "*Ich kahn nicht mehr halten.*" In English this translated, "I can't hold on any longer." Then his knee buckled and the human pyramid collapsed causing everyone to fall the great height, resulting in two deaths and serious and permanent injury to others in the Wallenda family. It was a tragic event that brought fear and deep compassionate concern to the hundreds of spectators gathered there in 1962.

---

[1] *Webster, New World Dictionary of the American Language* (Second College Edition). New York: Simon &Schuster, 1972, p. 1442.

The Wallendas had made their living *balancing*. At a later date Karl Wallenda died at the age of 73 following a plunge from the high wire stretched across a main thoroughfare from one high building to another in San Juan, Puerto Rico. He was nearly across the street, balancing on the wire using a long pole to help, when a sudden gust of wind caused him to lose his *balance* and fall to the pavement below. The fall caused Karl Wallenda's death.

Not all aspects of *balance* end up in death or bodily paralysis. *Balance* has its bright moments as well. On occasion, even humor brings a sparkle to the balance situation.

There is a story about a prominent family that hired a professional biographer to highlight the many achievements of its members. When the biographer discovered a "black sheep," who had been executed in the electric chair for murder, the family leaders "shifted" into damage control and asked the biographer if he could "balance" this account of Uncle George in such a way it would not reflect negatively on what otherwise was an outstanding family record. Many good and one bad, but the bad was so devastating that they reasoned it would be difficult indeed to get a "good balance."

The biographer assured them that he could take care of the problem with a little help from *semantics*. The end result produced this statement: "Uncle George occupied a chair of applied electronics at an important government institution. He was attached to this position by the strongest of ties, and his death came as a real shock."

If someone would ask me to name two outstanding Christians who do some very unpredictable things, make unprecedented remarks, and live joyful balanced lives, I would not hesitate for a moment. I would name Dallas Theological Seminary Practical Theologian Howard Hendricks and Eastern College's Sociologist Anthony Campolo. For example, Campolo ate with sinners like his Lord and Savior Jesus Christ when he sponsored an impromptu birthday party for prostitutes eating at a diner. As he gave Agnes a birthday cake, he *balanced* it with the Gospel which he clearly presented to the birthday girl and her friends.

As for Howie Hendricks, his escapades date back to his youth in Philadelphia where a sixth grade teacher told him, "I've heard all about you and I don't believe a word of it." This impressed him so deeply that this worldly delinquent became a changed person. While serving as a consultant to a "declining" church many years later, Professor Hendricks was asked by the Official Board of the church to make a recommendation as to what they could do. His response was, "Put a fence around it and charge admission so that people can come and see how church was done in the 1950's."[2] Who can count the number of lives that have been changed since that sixth grade experience by this creative and humble servant of the Lord and his wife Jeanne?

If there is one thing that can be attributed to the character formation of both these men it is *balance*—the beauty and strength of balanced motives, perspectives and actions. There must be *balance* between spiritual and moral values that are taught and those which are caught. It's "show and tell" in reverse.

Most mature married couples have an "ideal agenda" that reads like this: totally committed to my spouse, consistently reliable and responsible as a parent, faithful in my relationships with others, reasonably successful in the workplace of choice, and generously active in the neighborhood community. To make this ideal scenario happen requires a *balanced approach to life*. This balance is not easy to come by and must be "weighed" frequently. Even though it is not easy to acquire, it must be sought after and once attained satisfactorily, maintained diligently.

We need *balance* in all of our relationships of life, and in our time and energy commitments. We must constantly prioritize. *Ephesians 4:1* of the *New Testament*[3] counsels us to live worthy of the vocation to which we are called. The Greek word that is translated *worthy* is *axios*. That word has a relation to weights and measures. That which is *axios* balances the scales to good advantage. Our lives are worthy when they are in balance. We need to keep them that way. What say you?

---

[2] Iseley, Lee K. "They Are Coming To Us," *The Nor Easter*, Villanova, PA: American Missionary Fellowship, Winter 2005, p. 1.

[3] *New Testament*, Ephesians 4:1.

FIFTEEN

OOPS!

God never says "Oops" and never says "Wow." The reason is obvious. He never fails, and he is never taken by surprise.

I've made many mistakes, failed on numerous occasions, and said "Wow!" when I read "A Normal Boy marries an Oblong Girl." I had to read beyond the headlines of this Bloomington, Illinois newspaper in order to understand that both Normal and Oblong were communities in Illinois.

Does making a mistake have an effect upon our lives? It certainly does! Lloyd Ogilvie has pointed out that most of us "limp along fearful of repeating past mistakes."[1] He calls mistakes "stumbles" and claims that the malady is universal.

Failures come in numerous packages. There are "one-shot" failures, habitual failures, personality failures, relational failures, life-time goal failures, spiritual failures, and many more.

Causes of failures are multiple also. Some of the reasons why people fail are: (1) the tendency to push beyond the parameters of universal laws and good common sense; (2) the setting up of unrealistic expectations for ourselves; (3) the lack of motivation and the existence of weak resolve;(4) inadequate discipline in our lives; (5) the "win at any cost" syndrome; (6) the desire to impress; and many others.

---

[1] Ogilvie, Lloyd, *Lord of Loose Ends*. Dallas: Word Publishing, 1991, p.156.

For sixteen years I was a chaplain at Michigan State University in East Lansing, Michigan. During most of those years Duffy Daugherty was the colorful and successful coach of the MSU football team. In spite of his win record there was one rabid fan who sat on the forty-yard line, about 30 yards above the playing field, who doubted Daugherty's ability to call the right plays. This fan was "gifted" with an exceptionally loud voice. He kept yelling at the coach to abandon his line plays and go into a passing game.

On the occasion when Michigan State was playing the University of Iowa in a very dull scoreless first half our fan, who found more excitement in watching wet paint dry, shouted repeatedly to Daugherty to pass the ball. Finally the quarterback Earl Morrill faded back with the ball hidden on his hip and passed the football to Gene Washington as Washington raced down the sidelines. Washington caught the pass and gained 32 yards. The fan quickly stood to his feet, cupped his hands, and shouted "Okay Duffy, good play! I've got to go now. From here on you're on your own."

I'm glad God does not say that to us when we do not do the right thing, or hesitate to obey His commands. In fact, He does the opposite. He not only promises to never leave us, nor forsake us,[2] but he informs us that a just person may fail many times and shall get up and get going again.[3] The challenge is that no matter how many times we fail we can bounce back, so we do not quit.

The message not to quit was vividly illustrated by an experience that the famous Ignace Jan Paderewski had many years ago. Here's the story as told by Charles Swindoll.

"Ignace Jan Paderewski, the famous Polish pianist and statesman, was once scheduled to perform at a great concert hall in America. It was a black-tie affair—a high society extravaganza.

"Present in the audience that evening was a woman who had brought her nine-year-old son, hoping that he would be encouraged to practice the piano if he could just hear the great Paderewski at the keyboard. Weary of waiting for the concert to begin, and being there against his wishes anyway,

---

[2] *New Testament*, Hebrews 13:5.
[3] *Old Testament*, Proverbs 24:16

the lad squirmed restlessly in his seat. Then, as his mother turned to talk with friends, the boy slipped out of his seat and down the aisle, strangely drawn to the ebony concert grand sitting majestically and alone at the center of the huge stage. He sat down on the tufted leather stool, placed his small hands on the black-and-white keys and began to play "Chop Sticks."

"Suddenly the crowd hushed, and hundreds of frowning faces turned in his direction. Irritated and embarrassed, some began to shout, 'Hey, get that boy away from there!' 'Where's his mother?' 'Somebody stop him!'

"Backstage, Paderewski heard the uproar and the sound of the simple tune. When he saw what was happening, he hurried onto the stage. Without a word to the audience, he walked up behind the lad, reached his arms around either side of him, and began to improvise a countermelody. As the two made music together, the master pianist kept whispering into the boy's ear, 'Keep going. Don't quit, son. Keep on playing...don't stop...don't quit.'"

Swindoll adds: "So it is with us. We hammer away at life day by day, and sometimes it seems about as insignificant as 'Chop Sticks.' Then, about the time we are ready to give up, along comes the master, who leans over and whispers, 'Don't quit. Keep going,' as He provides His divine countermelody of grace, love, and joy at just the right moment."[4]

So says Charles Swindoll. What say you?

---

[4] Swindoll, Charles, *Day By Day*. Nashville, TN, W Publishing Group, a Division of Thomas Nelson, Inc., 2000, Introduction.

SIXTEEN

MAPS

Maps are like people. They come in all shapes and sizes. Perhaps that statement is not fair to maps. After all, maps are somewhat contained and limited in size and scope.

Mapmaking is done by cartographers who are professionally involved in the study and practice of making maps and globes. The word *cartography* emerges from two Greek words, *chartis* and *graphein*. The former means *map* and the latter means *write*.

The oldest known map dates back to the Golden Age of Greece, the 5th century B. C. They were basically topographical in nature. Since this rather crude beginning in the sphere of cartography, modern technology has brought about dramatic changes to meet new generational demands. The computer has revolutionized mapmaking. Today's quality maps are made with software that is highly specialized.

Maps function as visualization tools for distinct directions and spatial data. These tools are stored in databases with the movement away from analog to digital methods of mapmaking.

There are many different types of maps. There are *road maps* used to plan trips and to give directions en route. There are *topographical maps* which give the shape and elevations of areas under consideration. There are *physical maps* which show mountains, rivers, and lakes and other physical features.

There are *climate maps* that offer information about the climatic conditions and precipitation in various regions. There are *political, economic* and *resource maps* that give specialized information. There are *thematic, census, historical,* and *satellite maps* and many more. Most maps include a compass rose which shows which direction is north, south, east and west.

I have never met an adult person who has not depended upon and used maps, not once, but many times to provide information that is desired or necessary. My mother, for example, was an avid map reader. She would read maps for hours at a time. Even though she did not travel that much physically before the time of her death, she "traveled" in her mind around the world and into outer space frequently.

One day, after concentrating on a map of Michigan, she surprised me by saying, "Son, do you know that there is a place in our country where you have to go *south* rather than north in order to get into Canada?"

"That's hard to believe, Mother," I replied, as all the exit places that I knew of required a journey northward to get to Canada.

"Please look with me at this map," she said. I did, and sure enough, if you were in the city of Detroit, Michigan and wanted to travel to Windsor, Ontario, Canada through the tunnel or over the Ambassador Bridge, your route would be going almost due south. Without the benefit of that map to confirm this I would not have believed that fact to be true. Once in Windsor you go northward again.

This experience opened up a plethora of insights to me. How often on "*God's map*" for our lives He finds it necessary to "send us south before we can go north" in order to accomplish His will for us. I thanked my mother for revealing this to me and I could see she was pleased that she had "stretched" my concept of the importance of maps.

I recall a time when I would have given a lot for a map of the terrain in the heavily forested and mountainous area of northwestern Pennsylvania. As I wandered in circles while darkness was approaching, it was close to "panic time" when I heard rifle shots being fired a long distance away. Firing my gun in response I began to stumble in the direction where the shots came from thinking that my hunting buddies were trying to find me. We finally got together for a reunion I shall long remember.

This harrowing experience taught me a great never-to-be-forgotten lesson that I should only travel in unfamiliar territory in the future with a flashlight, a compass, and a map. *Maps* are extremely important. What say you?

SEVENTEEN

SECULAR HUMANISM

Modern secular humanists cannot comprehend the centrality of religion, Christianity in particular, in our American culture in these United States. This is true in spite of the finding of the Pew Research Council in March 2002, which determined that 82 percent of Americans claim to be Christians.[1]

Let's take a moment to clarify the terms of *secularism* and *humanism*. *Secularism* is a system of doctrines and practices that either disregards or totally rejects any form of religious faith and worship. It wants no intrusion of religion into the affairs of state or public life. It's as simple as that. *Humanism* is a modern, non-theistic, and rationalistic movement that adheres to the belief that man is capable by himself to self-fulfillment, without any dependence on supernatural interference. Place these two basic concepts into a person's belief system and you have a *modern secular humanist*.

Even though secular humanists represent a comparatively small minority of the American populace, they rely upon the intensive influence of liberal judges in our courts, atheistic professors in academia, special interest groups, and prominent leaders in some of the media. It is no longer a subtle and covert infiltration; it is an out-and-out declaration of war by people like Dr. Michael Newdow to eliminate any and all references to God, and to abolish every symbol that is associated with our Creator in our nationalistic public life.

---

[1] Gingrich, Newt, *Winning The Future*. Washington, DC: Regnery Publishing, Inc., 2005, p. 55.

What is most surprising is that while the secular humanists attempt to put this nation under siege, the majority of Americans, whose views are diametrically opposed to theirs, are either complacent, threatened, or waiting for someone else to engage in the battle. Edmund Burke's words were never more timely, "All that is necessary for the triumph of evil is that good men do nothing."[2]

Our Constitution begins with the words, "We the people..." We the people need to act now, on the grass-roots levels, to stand up for what Thomas Jefferson describes as our "unalienable Rights" when he declared that "All men...are endowed by their Creator with certain unalienable Rights... among them are Life, Liberty, and the Pursuit of Happiness."[3]

Our Bill of Rights is a strong document that was designed by our Founding Fathers to protect freedom *of* religion, not freedom *from* religion. We must *not* be intimidated by a small minority of secular humanists with a loud voice who wish to destroy that which has made our country great—our faith in a higher being, our belief in God.

No one can logically deny that our nation does have a strong national religious diversity. This, however, in no logical way nullifies the fact that from our inception our country has been "a nation under God." One nation under God is as inclusive as possible. It transcends any one faith. *Pluralism does not mean paganism!*

George Washington, our first president, on the occasion of his first inauguration on April 30, 1789, with his right hand on the Bible bent forward and kissed that Bible because, as he stated, "It would be peculiarly improper to omit in this first official act my fervent supplications to that Almighty Being who rules over the universe."[4]

When 56 very brave men met in Philadelphia, Pennsylvania on August 2, 1776 to sign a new document that had been adopted on July 4, that Declaration of Independence was a partnership between the living and the dead and the yet unborn. The last sentence of the final paragraph of

---

[2] Mead, Frank S., *12,000 Religious Quotations*. Grand Rapids, MI: Baker Book House, 1989, p. 125.
[3] *Ibid.*, p. 176.
[4] Gingrich, *op. cit.*, p. 49.

that parchment reads: "And for the support of this declaration, with a firm reliance on the protection of divine providence, we mutually pledge to each other our lives, our fortunes and our sacred honor." To them *liberty* was more important than *security*. They took the risk and paid a high price while relying on the protection of God to do so.

Thomas Jefferson, our third president, is often thought of as the modern secular humanist's "champion," because he expressed his opinion in a letter written to the Danbury Baptists on January 1, 1802 that there should be "a wall of separation between church and state."[5] This was his opinion at that time, not an official edict. The secular humanists ignore the fact that Jefferson attended church services regularly, and that his statement on the Jefferson Memorial reads: "I have sworn upon the altar of God eternal hostility against every form of tyranny over the mind of man."[6]

Jefferson signed bills to appropriate financial support for chaplains in Congress and in the armed services. He urged military personnel to "attend divine services." He encouraged the teaching of religion at the University of Virginia which he helped to establish. He proposed that the Rotunda be used for chapel services. Concerning the Bible he wrote, "I have always said, I always say, that the studious perusal of the sacred volume will make better citizens, better fathers, and better husbands."[7] In regard to Jesus Christ, Jefferson wrote, "I hold the precepts of Jesus as delivered by himself, to be the most pure, benevolent, and sublime which have ever been preached to man."[8] Concerning morality in public life, Jefferson penned, "Of all the systems of morality, ancient and modern, which have come under my observation, none appear so pure to me as that of Jesus."[9] Some *champion* for modern secular humanists, wouldn't you say!

It was Abraham Lincoln, thought by many to be our greatest president, who said in his famous Gettysburg Address: "...that this nation, under God, shall have a new birth of freedom; and that government of the people, by the people, for the people shall not perish from the earth."[10] It is good to

[5] *Ibid.*, p. 50.

[6] *Ibid.*, p. 51.

[7] Mead, *op. cit.*, p. 29.

[8] *Ibid.*, p. 54.

[9] *Ibid.*, p. 64.

[10] Gingrich, *op. cit.*, p. 55.

read and reread these lines in the light of the fact that the secular humanists have an agenda to help make sure that God does "perish from the earth," especially in our national life.

President Lincoln underscored two very important concepts in that statement. They are: (1) the fact that our nation is "under God," that God is the Supreme and Sovereign Being; and, (2) that the people really count! It is time for the people of our nation to rise up and be counted upon to protest against those who desire to take God out of our public lives. Small wonder that President Lincoln endorsed the role of the churches in our public life so graciously when he uttered these words, "Bless all the churches, and blessed be God, who, in this great trial, giveth us the churches."[11]

A word of serious caution to the modern secular humanists who wish to deny us *freedom of religion* in the public square of life. The word comes from President Lincoln who said: "Those who deny freedom to others deserve it not for themselves, and, under a just God, cannot long retain it."[12]

When our Congress adopted the phrase "one nation under God, " and President Dwight D. Eisenhower signed it, polls indicated that it had an approval rating of 91 percent among American people. They wanted this phrase in their Pledge of Allegiance by an overwhelming majority. When will this small minority of secular humanists wise up to the fact that their views are not the mainstream of American society and that Jefferson's expressed "opinion" to the Danbury Baptists is not in the Constitution!

Secular humanists may depend upon the reflections of Hobbes, Hume, Voltaire, Darwin, Freud, Russell, Nietzsche, Rousseau, Huxley and others for their godless philosophies of relativism, subjectivism, atheism, determinism, hedonism, materialism, nihilism, postmodernism, secularism and humanism. Most of us in America prefer to look to our Founding Fathers and national leaders who espoused a recognition of the deity of our Creator and a dependence upon Him for wisdom, protection and provision. What say you?

---

[11] Mead, *op. cit.*, p. 79.
[12] *Ibid.*, p. 152.

EIGHTEEN

HEARTACHES

Not everyone enjoys cowboy lyrics or country music but, without a question, Dwight Yoakam hit it big when he pointed out three heartaches and started his chorus with the words: "Now I've got heartaches by the number, troubles by the score." As soon as I hummed the music to this ballad, I remembered an earlier song that was popular when I was younger that started out with "Heartaches, heartaches..." giving more than two syllables to both words.

That song was sung by Patsy Cline, the small-town West Virginia girl with the sultry voice who made it big in the music world, in films and Broadway shows before her tragic death in an airplane crash while she was still young. She brought country music to the mainstream, helped greatly by her rendition of these words:

Heartaches, heartaches,
My loving you meant only heartaches,
Your kiss was such a sacred thing to me,
I can't believe it's just a burning memory.

Heartaches, heartaches,
What does it matter how my heart breaks?
I should be happy with some one new
But my heart aches for you.[1]

[1] Written by Al Hoffman and John Klenner. Released by Patsy Cline on October 8, 1962.

Headaches are bad, but *heartaches* are worse! If you have a severe heartache it should be for a good purpose. Bob Pierce, founder of both World Vision and the Samaritan's Purse, placed these words in the flyleaf of his well-worn Bible, *"Let my heart be broken by the things that break the heart of God."* There could be no better purpose than that!

George Herbert caught a vision of the heart in relation to a broken altar when he penned these lines: "A broken altar, Lord, thy servant rears, made of a heart and cemented with tears."[2] And who can reflect upon the words of Henry Wadsworth Longfellow's, "It's too late! Ah, nothing is too late, Till the tired heart shall cease to palpitate,"[3] without feeling the emotion he expressed? The tired heart, with its many heartaches throughout life's journeys, has hope unto the very end of one's physical existence.

When Jacob heard that his son, Joseph, had been killed he tore his clothes, put on sackcloth, and mourned many days.[4] This was deep mourning. Later, however, he learned that Joseph's life had been spared. Likewise, David suffered a severe heartache when he learned that King Saul was dead. He wept bitterly and fasted.[5]

Joni Eareckson Tada, who suffered with many heartaches through the nightmare of a severe accident that paralyzed much of her body, wrote, "There are days when my soul feels windblown, raw and exposed—many times when I'm tossed in a blustery tempest with everything breaking loose. But the God Who brings beauty out of blizzards promises to bring peace after the storm. And when the beauty dawns, I hardy remember the fright of that stormy trial."[6]

There is light at the end of the tunnel for those who suffer *heartaches*. Remember that joy comes with the morning.[7] Take the weapons of enduring faith and indescribable love against the sea of trouble and your distress will be lightened. It may end!

---

[2] *Seniors' Devotional Bible, New International Version.* Grand Rapids, MI: Zondervan Publishing House, 1995, p. 216.

[3] *Ibid.*, p. 252.

[4] *Old Testament*, Genesis 37:34.

[5] *Ibid.*, Second Samuel 1:11 and 12.

[6] *Seniors' Devotional Bible, op. cit.*, p. 393.

[7] *Old Testament*, Psalm 30:5.

As Charles Haddon Spurgeon, prince of preachers, writes: "There is One Who cares for you. His eye is on you. His heart beats with pity for the difficulties you face, and His omnipotent hand will bring you help. The darkest cloud will scatter in showers of mercy. The blackest night will give way to morning. If you are His, He will bind your wounds and heal your broken heart. Don't doubt His grace because of your trials. He loves you as much in times of trouble as in days of happiness."[8]

How meaningful are the paraphrased words of *First Peter 5:6 and 7* by J. B. Phillips: "So, humble yourselves under God's strong hand, and in good time He will lift you up. You can throw the whole weight of your anxieties upon Him, for you are His personal concern."[9] How soothing are the hope-filled expressions of the song writer, Jeremiah E. Rankin, "Are you weary, are you heavy hearted? Tell it to Jesus, Tell it to Jesus, Are you grieving over joys departed? Tell it to Jesus alone."[10]

Very few ministers of the Gospel experienced more heartaches than the late A. W. Tozer, Christian Missionary Alliance pastor in Chicago for many years and, yet, he wrote these succinct words, "With the goodness of God to desire our highest welfare, the wisdom of God to plan it and the power of God to achieve it, what do we lack? Surely we are the most favored of all creatures."[11]

If Mrs. Tada, Songwriter Rankin, and Pastors Charles Haddon Spurgeon and A. W. Tozer can say these things concerning *heartaches*, what say you?

[8] *Seniors' Devotional Bible, op. cit.,* p. 425.
[9] Phillips, J. B., *The New Testament in Modern English.* London: Geoffrey Bles, 1960, p. 493.
[10] Rankin, Jeremiah E. and Lorenz, Edmund S., *Tell It to Jesus.* (Found in most hymn books).
[11] *Ibid.,* p. 778.

NINETEEN

SMALL THINGS

A phrase often repeated is "Don't sweat the small stuff." The message is clear. Do not get overly-excited about those things that appear to be of minor importance. Save your time, energy, and adrenaline for the more important things of life.

Anxiety is undue concern about the *unknown* in our lives. *Worry* is concern about the *known*. We do not know the outcome of some impending event so we "cross that bridge" many times before we come to it and over-anxiety controls our actions. We cannot pay a bill due in a day or two because of our limited financial resources at that moment. We know what the problem is and find ourselves almost paralyzed with worry. Usually when we put things into proper perspective we find ways of overcoming both anxiety and worry and can spend our time and energy by focusing on ways to solve the problem. That way we do not have to "sweat the small stuff."

When an acquaintance talked about "boulders in his shoes," he was asked to explain. His response was, "Well, I've got some worries that seem big but, actually, they are not big at all. They feel like boulders but when I take off my shoes I find that they are small pebbles. It's amazing that such things could *seem* so large."

Why is it that small things have such power to hassle us? Is it the threat of urgency? Can it be due to a series of events or disappointments that cause us to reach the point where one more "small thing" is like the proverbial

71

straw that broke the camel's back? Is self-pity a factor in the equation? Does insecurity lead to immaturity in coping with the lesser things of life? Is it a loss of confidence in God's power to provide strength and wisdom to help us to overcome undue concern about the smaller things in life? Are we physically exhausted and emotionally drained because of some changes in our lifestyles?

Not all trouble can be eliminated as quickly as we would like. *Job* testifies to that. Not all needs can be met. Not all pain can be ended. Some cancers cannot be healed. When we are up against the "biggies" in our lives, we must eliminate as much of the small clutter as possible. It will "eat us up" if we don't. We are talking survival. We can heed the words of the songwriter and begin by attempting to "accentuate the positive and eliminate the negative."

Small stuff can have a big effect on our attitudes and actions in life. Have you ever moved? If you plan to downsize in your move, perhaps from a four-bedroom home to a two-bedroom condo you know the process of sorting through accumulated stuff in preparation for a yard sale and truckloads of "things" to be given to the Salvation Army. We need "housecleaning" periodically in our minds to establish what is important and what is not. Don't wait until company comes to get rid of the "small stuff" that has lost much of its value, need and attraction. *Simplify your stock; get rid of the small things!*

That famous "Author Unknown" penned these words:

> Said the robin to the sparrow,
> I should really like to know,
> Why these anxious human beings
> Rush about and worry so.
>
> Said the sparrow to the robin,
> I think that it must be
> They have no heavenly Father
> Such as cares for you and me.[1]

---

[1] Wagner, Charles U., *Winning Words For Daily Living*. Grand Rapids, MI: Kregel Publications, 1989, p. 21.

Consider Jesus' words, "Look at the birds of the air; they do not sow or reap or store away in barns, and yet your heavenly Father feeds them. Are you not much more valuable than they? Who of you by worrying can add a single hour to his life?"[2] This is what Jesus said. What say you?

---

[2] *New Testament*, Matthew 6:26 and 27.

TWENTY

SIMPLE

Aaron Copland, born in Brooklyn, NY in 1900, was a musical composer, conductor, writer, teacher and lecturer whose music was distinctively American and played well on radio especially. He has a long relationship with the Boston Symphony Orchestra and its conductor Serge Koussevitzky, who was himself a strong advocate of modern American music.

Copland had resolved early in his career to express his ideas in the simplest possible terms. This concept of his is especially prominent in the music he wrote for a ballet entitled *Appalachian Spring*. In the seventh section of this ballet he used authentic folk material. The folk tune he composed featured a pioneer celebration in springtime of a newly-built farmhouse in Pennsylvania for a bride-to-be and a young farmer who was to become her husband.

The tune emerged from the words of a Shaker hymn, "The Gift To Be Simple," which highlighted the Shaker religious sect that held strong community values and an amazingly simple lifestyle. The lyrics of the hymn went like this:

'Tis the gift to be simple,
'Tis the gift to be free,
'Tis the gift to come down
Where we ought to be.
And when we find ourselves
In the place just right,

'Twill be in the valley of
Love and Delight.[1]

A "simple lifestyle" in our highly sophisticated, pressure-packed, "hurry and harried" way of living is hard to find, if not impossible to achieve. The words that best describe today's society in America are these:

This is the age
Of the half page
And the quick hash
And the mad dash
The bright night
With nerves tight
The plane hop
And the brief stop
The lamp tan
In the short span
The big shot
In a good spot
And the brain strain
And the heart pain
And the cat naps
'till the spring snaps
that ends the fun
for life is done.[2]

Perhaps what we need is a few more trips on Vance Havner's "slow train" that stops to pick up milk cans at each of the dairy farms, and gives us the opportunity to view the peaceful countryside with all its natural splendor.

A lesson can be learned from an experience in the life of Christian Friedrich Theodore Steinway, son of Henry Engelhard Steinway. Henry, the father, was a master cabinet maker. He built his first piano in his home in Seesen, Germany. By the time he founded his firm in 1853 he was an immigrant to the United States and had five sons: Henry, Jr., Albert, C. F.

---

[1] Daniels, Arthur and Wagner, Lavern, *music*. New York: Holt, Rinehart and Winston, 1975, p. 399.
[2] Braiser, Virginia, *Time of the Mad Atom*. Quoted in numerous publications and can be found in *Day By Day* by Charles Swindoll and published by Thomas Nelson, Inc., 2000, p. 275.

Theodore, William and Charles. Theodore was the "scientist" in the family. He used many of the acoustical theories advanced by the renowned physicist Hermann von Heimholtz.

Because of his great expertise and his contributions to the manufacture of these majestic Steinway grand pianos, which by the latter part of the 1860's had produced many hundreds of grand pianos, Christian Friedrich Theodore Steinway was honored by Oberlin College in Ohio, founded in 1833, with an honorary doctorate. On that same occasion he was given an unusual plaque which read, "*Out of great tension comes harmony.*" The rationale for the statement on this plaque emerged from the fact that while there were 40,000 pounds of pressure exerted on the 243 strings on each of Steinway "grands," these pianos "looked" so serene as they simply graced their various locales.

If our lives are like a lesson in grammar where we find the present *tense* and the past *perfect*, we need to slow down and smell the roses. Could it be that we need a more simple lifestyle? Can we believe that out of great tension can come harmony? What say you?

TWENTY – ONE

BOOMERANG

Boomerang. That word has a nice ring to it. It also has quite a unique history.

Historical "purists" want to make sure we do not confuse the *throwing wood or stick* with *boomerang*. The throwing wood was basically a hunting weapon. There is a slight difference between the *throwing wood* and the *throwing stick*. The throwing stick is a straight rod of hardwood which rotates while flying and is usually sharpened at both ends.

The *boomerang*, subject of this chapter, is an aerodynamically shaped throwing variant of the throwing wood that is used primarily for sports activities where a return throw is required. Boomerangs originally were carved from naturally-bent hardwood where the grain could follow the proper angle to give it the strength needed. Today, because of the development of strong materials and quality glues, the design limitations and other restrictions have been eliminated. Boomerangs are now made in a great variation of styles and colors and are widely available to the public. In fact, many adorn the walls of restaurants for decorative purposes.

It is generally assumed that boomerangs originated in Australia. Researchers believe, however, that they were invented in India. The only thing certain about their origin is that their origin is uncertain. An influence from the ancient Orient is most likely. It is a fact that evidence of throwing woods have been found in such remotes places as Poland, Holland, Scandinavia, India, Egypt and Australia—even in Arizona—in prehistoric time.

It took the Aborigines of Australia to refine the boomerang and increase its accuracy in returning to the thrower. The Aborigines developed unique and outstanding skills in both their manufacture and their use. In fact, the late Joe Trimbey of Botany Bay in New South Wales was so skillful with the use of the boomerang that on one occasion before the presence of the Queen of England in 1954 he had ten boomerangs in the air simultaneously. Some of these boomerangs he would catch with his feet.

I chose this subject matter because the boomerang is symbolically an instrument designed to demonstrate that when you throw something away from you it will return back to you.

The Apostle Paul spoke of *bread* symbolically when he referred to the "unleavened bread of sincerity and truth."[1] In another passage of Scripture we read, "Cast your bread on the surface of the waters, for you will find it after many days."[2] Jesus elaborated on this "return theme" when he spoke these words. "...and he who receives a righteous man in the name of a righteous man shall receive a righteous man's reward."[3] *Mark* shortens Jesus' statement by writing, "For whoever gives you a cup of water to drink because of your name as *followers* of Christ, truly I say to you, he shall not lose his reward."[4]

Presupposing the motive is selflessness and the spirit is generous, the "boomerang of God's goodness" will return to the sender or the giver. Let me illustrate this by describing a moving story told by Leith Anderson in his thought-provoking book entitled, *Becoming Friends With God.*

Moses Mendelssohn was the grandfather of the famous German musical composer Felix. Moses Mendelssohn was not a handsome man, and he knew it. He was very short in stature, and he had a back deformity that in that day was called "humpback." He took a business trip to visit a merchant in the German city of Hamburg. While he was

---

[1] *New Testament*, First Corinthians 5:8.

[2] *Old Testament*, Ecclesiastes 11:1.

[3] *New Testament*, Matthew 10:42.

[4] *Ibid.*, Mark 9:41.

there he met the beautiful daughter of the merchant. Frumtje was her name. He was enthralled by her, but she'd have nothing to do with him. She was repulsed by his appearance. After several days of attempting conversation with her, he got up his courage for one last attempt. He spoke to her. But she didn't answer. She never looked his way. In a last attempt, he asked her a question, "Do you believe marriages are made in heaven?"

She didn't look at him, but she answered him, "Yes. Do you believe marriages are made in heaven?"

Moses Mendelssohn answered, "Yes, I do. You see, in heaven at the birth of each boy, the Lord announces which girl he will marry. When I was born, my future bride was pointed out to me. Then the Lord added, 'But your wife will be humpbacked.' Right then and there I called out, 'Oh, Lord, a humpbacked woman would be a tragedy. Please, Lord, give me the hump and let her be beautiful.'" According to the story, Frumtje looked into his eyes and then reached out her hand and touched him. Something deep inside of her had been stirred. She gave him her hand and later became his lifelong wife.[5]

What a *boomerang* that was! What say you?

---

[5] Anderson, Leith, *Becoming Friends With God*. Minneapolis, MN: Bethany House, 2001, pp. 271-272.

TWENTY – TWO

TOMORROW

Broadway's award-winning musical *Annie* produced many "singable" tunes. Among these favorites was the hit song *Tomorrow*, with lyrics by Martin Charmin and music by Charles Strouse.

It was a common scenario for an amateur singer to burst out with the lines, "Tomorrow! Tomorrow! I love ya Tomorrow! You're always a day away!"

Tomorrow is a popular theme in life. Soren Kierkegaard wrote, "What is anxiety? It is the next day."[1] Lloyd John Ogilve opined, "Most of us get so tomorrow-oriented that we do not enjoy the present moment. We are preoccupied by what is coming, and we fail to experience what is."[2]

Sir Winston Churchill invoked this piece of wisdom, "It is a mistake to look too far ahead. Only one link in the chain of destiny can be handled at a time."[3]

Jesus told us to concentrate on today, allowing tomorrow to be another opportunity. These are His words, "Therefore do not worry about tomorrow,

---

[1] Ogilvie, Lloyd J., *God's Best For My Life*. Eugene, Oregon: Harvest Home Publishers, p. 239.
[2] *Ibid.*

[3] Palmer, Arnold, *Golf Journal*. Chicago: Triumph Books, 1997, p. 126.

for tomorrow will worry about itself. Each day has enough trouble of its own."[4] Small wonder that William R. Inge warned, "Worry is interest paid on trouble before it comes due."[5]

Proverbs, the Biblical book of wise sayings, with its wisdom distilled into short phrases, records, "Do not boast about tomorrow, for you do not know what a day may bring forth."[6] The writer James of the *New Testament* captures the same idea in this statement, "Come now, you who say, 'Today or Tomorrow, we shall go to such and such a city, and spend a year there and engage in business and make a profit.' Yet you do not know what your life will be like tomorrow. You are *just* a vapor that appears for a little while and then vanishes away. Instead, you *ought* to say, 'If the Lord wills, we shall live and also do this or that.'"[7]

The ancient prophet Isaiah, who prophesied during the reigns of four of Israel's kings, characterized the pessimistic view of tomorrow held by many when he wrote, "...let us eat and drink, for tomorrow we may die."[8]

There is a powerful story told in the *Old Testament* book of *Second Kings* that encapsulates many of the themes expressed in the statements given previously. It occurs in Chapters 6 and 7 of this book. The setting was in the ancient city of Samaria around 850 B.C. At that time there was a great famine in this fortress city. Add to that, the city was under siege by the mighty forces of Ben-Hadad, King of Syria.

Conditions were so desperate in Samaria that a donkey's head was sold for 80 pieces of silver and some of the inhabitants had turned to cannibalism, eating their own children. It was a nasty and a very critical situation!

The plot thickens when we read that there were four lepers sitting at the entrance to the gate because they were not allowed in the city with the dread disease. They surveyed their dilemma. There was acute famine in the city. They were surrounded by a hostile enemy, and they were suffering

---

[4] *The NIV Serendipity Bible for Study Groups,* Matthew 6:34. Grand Rapids, MI: Zondervan Bible Publishers, 1989, p. 1248.

[5] Ogilvie, *op. cit.,* p. 232.

[6] *Old Testament,* Proverbs 27:1.

[7] *New Testament,* James 4:13-15.

[8] *Old Testament,* Isaiah 22:13.

from Hansen's disease awaiting a slow, painful death. This was not a bright tomorrow for them!

The account of this incident states that they reasoned, "...Why do we sit here until we die? If we say, 'We will enter the city.' Then the famine is in the city and we shall die there; and if we sit her we die also. Now therefore come, and let us go over to the camp of the Syrians. If they spare us, we shall live; and if they kill us we shall but die."[9]

Consequently, they went to the Syrian camp at twilight and much to their amazement there were no soldiers there. The camp was abandoned. The cause was due to an act of God that filled their camp with a thundering noise that made the Syrian host believe that the dreadful Hittites and the forces of Egypt were bearing down upon them to annihilate them. So they fled in fear leaving everything behind them. This is what the lepers discovered. There were no soldiers but there was all this spoil at their disposal.

The lepers ate till they could eat no more. They began to hide the treasures.[10] Then they started to reason together once more. The Scriptures inform us, "Then they said to one another, 'We are not doing right. This day is a day of good news, but we are keeping silent; if we wait until morning light, punishment will overtake us. Now therefore come, let us go and tell the king's household.'"[11]

When the king heard this astounding news he was leery and thought that it was a trick and a trap laid by the Syrians. He sent out an advance guard and discovered the truth. The Syrians had fled just as the prophet Elisha had indicated earlier that they would.

What happened confirmed the words spoken hundreds of years later by *James*, which are cited earlier in this chapter. You are now aware of what the scriptures and others have to say about *tomorrow*. What say you?

---

[9] *Old Testament,* Second Kings 7:3-4.

[10] *Ibid.,* verse 8.

[11] *Ibid.,* verse 9.

TWENTY – THREE

SERENDIPITY

Serendipity is the facility of making happy chance discoveries. That was the conclusion reached by the English author Horace Walpole (1717-1797) in 1743, when he was 26 years of age.[1]

Walpole also believed and forcefully stated, "Men are often capable of greater things than they perform."[2] This is somewhat in keeping with Physician Oliver Wendell Holmes, Senior's later comment that most people die with the music still in them.[3]

Horace Walpole flashed a sense of humor, something he was prone to so on more than one occasion, when he commented, "In my youth I thought of writing a satire on mankind, but now in my age I think I should write an apology for them."[4] He instructed his friends, "To act with common sense according to the moment is the best wisdom I know."[5]

I intend to follow his advice as I present some concepts of *serendipity* in this chapter.

---

[1] *The NIV Serendipity Bible for Study Guide,* Quotation Opposite Title Page. Grand Rapids, MI: Zonder-van Bible Publishers, 1989.

[2] *The New Dictionary of Thoughts.* New York: Standard Book Company, 1957, p. 1.

[3] Holmes, Oliver Wendell, Sr. *Quotations by Author by Michael Moncur's Cynical Quotations.* #26186. Can be found on the website.

[4] *The New Dictionary of Thoughts, op. cit.,* p. 81.

[5] *Ibid.,* p. 98.

Without a doubt, as Walpole spoke of *serendipity* he borrowed his idea from an old Persian fairy tale entitled, *The Three Princes of Serendip*. Serendip was a reference to Ceylon, formerly a British colony but now an independent democratic socialist republic with a parliamentary governmental structure. It is known as Sri Lanka today and is located on a tropical island off the southeastern tip of India. This small nation has a reputation for three things especially. It is the place of long standing civil war between the Sinhalese and the Tamil peoples; it is the location of one of the greatest tea growing areas in the world with their tender pekoe leaves; and, it is the home of the greatly respected and world-famous golfer, Vijay Singh.

In the fairy tale *The Three Princes of Serendip*, the princes has a knack, an aptitude for making fortunate discoveries accidentally. From personal experience, let me give two illustrations I shall long remember and appreciate immensely.

In the last days of the month of May 1945 I was a grossly underweight and slightly anemic United States Army Air Force pilot just returned state-side from the prisoner-of-war camp, Stalag 6-G in northwest Germany. I weighed about 120 pounds, 90 pounds less than my normal weight at that time. My nervous system was trying hard to adjust to my "home environment," and my digestive system was attempting to cope with the common ingredients of food. It was "transition time" and among those offering aid in my hometown of Corning, New York was my pastor, Dr. Arthur B. Whiting.

Dr. Whiting suggested I take a couple of days and journey with him to what is now known as Davis College in Johnson City, New York, a school founded by Dr. John A. Davis in 1900. He was asked to give the Baccalaureate sermon at the college that year. With an agenda that was "open," I thought that his suggestion was a good one. I agreed to go with him. Moreover, my sister Joyce, was a student in the Junior class at Davis at that time so I would be able to be with her for this special time as well.

Then the *serendipitous moment* occurred. I would not rule out divine providence also in the "facility of making chance discoveries." One of the graduating Seniors, an honor student and the soloist for the Commencement Program, was Ruth Evelyn Snyder from Altoona, Pennsylvania. When I saw her beauty, both spiritually and physically, and witnessed her poise and charisma, and heard many complimentary comments about her integrity from the other students, it was "love at first sight" for this 23 year-old who knew in his heart that this was the girl he was looking for to be his wife.

Without going into detail about her believing that this was a *serendipitous moment* for her, certainly a very important part of the equation, let me conclude that this *serendipity* by saying we were married soon after, and are actually more in love with each other now than we were the day we were married in 1945. That is God's gift to us after more than sixty years of marriage, which included rearing two children, witnessing the birth of four granddaughters, and surviving a few severe physical testings along the way.

On a lighter note, let me share a second *serendipity*. It occurred after one of my many return trips from Singapore, where I served as a guest lecturer. Ruth was at the Philadelphia airport upon my arrival to take me home. She recognized my tiredness, but mentioned that a certain large electric fan was on sale in the King of Prussia Complex of many stores. That was the last day of the special price. Would I want to stop en route home? I agreed. We did. I bought the fan. As we were leaving Bloomingdale's I spotted a box, already overstuffed with slips of paper. There was a sign offering a free weekend for two in New York City with a four-day stay in a large four-room suite in the Marriott Marquis Hotel at Broadway and 45th Street in Time Square, pairs of tickets for three off-Broadway shows, a Sunday brunch at the Tavern on the Green in Central Park West and some other amenities, along with first-class round trip airfares and limousine service.

Hurriedly, I grabbed an application form and wrote down our names, address, phone number, and answered a question that was asked. I wadded up the paper and stuffed it in the box knowing the futility of what I was doing since the only thing I had ever won up to that point in my life was a Little Orphan Annie book at the age of 10.

Several weeks later while ministering in a Bible Conference at the Arden, North Carolina Presbyterian Church, pastored by the Reverend Ed Graham, Billy Graham's cousin, I received a surprise phone call from "Karen at Bloomingdale's in New York City." You guessed it! It was *serendipity!* Ruth and I won this trip, had a most memorable experience in New York City and "watched" as that Little Orphan Annie book paled into insignificance. This was a *serendipitous moment deluxe.*

As I give account of these two remarkable and memorable occasions, knowing there were others as well, I can only imagine that in *your* lifetime as a reader of this chapter you, too, have experienced some outstanding *serendipities.* What say you?

TWENTY – FOUR

OH, REALLY?

We first met when he was the senior pastor of a church in Bethlehem, Pennsylvania. Since then I have followed his career closely. Among other major accomplishments, he served as the senior pastor of the well-known First Presbyterian Church of Hollywood, California. He served as the chaplain of the United States Senate for years. He has written more than forty books, excelled as a television speaker, and has made his native country of Scotland proud. He is Dr. Lloyd John Ogilvie.

In his book, *God's Best for My Life*[1] which is a daily inspirational book designed for a deeper walk with God, Dr. Ogilvie cites a rather unusual incident best understood in his own words:

> Some years ago, when the science of voice amplification was in its infancy, a church I was serving equipped me with a remotely controlled lavaliere microphone with no cords attached. A power pack, which I wore in my hip pocket, was fed through an FM sending set which broadcast my voice on the public address system of the sanctuary. That gave me freedom to move about in the chancel and in the pulpit and be heard by the people. What was not known was that the same band on the FM dial had been assigned also to some ham radio operators.
>
> One Sunday I finished my sermon with a flourish, with my hand outstretched in a triumphant gesture. At that very moment a ham

---

[1] Ogilvie, Lloyd John, *God's Best For My Life*, Eugene, Oregon: Harvest Home Publishers, 1981.

radio operator was carrying on a conversation which invaded the public address system in the sanctuary. As I stood before my people finishing my sermon, his voice was heard over all the sanctuary. "Oh really?" he said to the person with whom he was carrying on a conversation. We all laughed.[2]

Dr. Ogilvie brought his humorous illustration to summation with the cogent comment, "'Oh, really?' points us to the credibility gap of what we say so eloquently." It actually is an *integrity issue* in the final analysis.

This is demonstrated vividly in the apparent "feud" that exists between Bill O'Reilly, the reigning king of cable news on the Fox News Network, and one of his challenging accusers, Peter Hart. Bill O'Reilly's very popular program, "The O'Reilly Factor," is lampooned by Peter Hart in his book, *The Oh Really? Factor.*[3] Each doubts strongly the *integrity* of the other and is quick to denounce with sarcasm statements made as patently false. In the process it would appear to some others and myself that O'Reilly takes the higher road and Hart, supported by Al Franken and Michael Moore, takes a lower road. What is certain is that the main issue is *integrity.*

Beverly Hamilton in an Ezine article on the website entitled; *I'm Too Busy—Oh Really?*,[4] makes her thesis a matter of integrity as well. The thrust of her argument is "Are you too busy being busy or busy being productive?" She asks further, "Is busyness your excuse for poor time management?" To her, the burden of proof lies in the realm of integrity.

The *integrity issue involves* all of us. Warren Wiersbe, for example, had the Christian church in mind when he wrote, "One of the church fathers said that the church was something like Noah's ark: if it weren't for the judgment on the outside, you could never stand the smell on the inside."[5]

Wiersbe goes on to ask the question, "What is integrity?"[6]

---

[2] *Ibid.*, p. 267.

[3] Hart, Peter, *The Oh Really? Factor: Unspinning Fox News Channel's Bill O'Reilly.* New York: Seven Stories Press, 2003.

[4] Hamilton, Beverly, Article *I'm Too Busy—Oh Really?* This appeared on Website as http:EzineArticles. com/. She also has written a book entitled *Is Busyness Affecting Your Business?*

[5] Wiersbe, Warren W., *The Integrity Crisis.* Nashville, Tennessee: Thomas Nelson Publishers, 1988, p. 11.

[6] *Ibid.*, p. 21.

He answers his question with a reference to the *Oxford English Dictionary* and makes this observation, "The word comes from the Latin *integritas* which means 'wholeness,' 'entireness,' 'completeness.' The root word is *integer* which means 'untouched,' 'intact,' 'entire.' Integrity is to personal or corporate character what health is to the body, or 20/20 vision is to the eyes. A person with integrity is not divided (that's *duplicity*), or merely pretending (that's *hypocrisy*). He, or she, is 'whole'; life is put together and things are working harmoniously. People with *integrity* have nothing to hide and nothing to fear. Their lives are open books. The are *integers*."[7]

With that concept of *integrity* in mind, we can add two tips that are found in Dr. Genie Z. Laborde's book, *Influencing Integrity*.[8] She writes, "Only human beings have integrity,"[9] and "Integrity implies a soundness that can be moral or amoral, but not immoral."[10]

So, when someone responds by saying, "Oh, really?", that person is laying it on the line as a personal challenge to either your personal integrity or the statement that you have made. The fewer "Oh, really's?" we encounter in life the more likely we will be "whole" persons avoiding duplicity, hypocrisy, manipulation, and rationalization. What say you?

---

[7] *Ibid.*

[8] Laborde, Genie Z., *Influencing Integrity*. Palo Alto, California: Syntony Publishing, 1983, p. 192.

[9] *Ibid.*, p. 195.

[10] *Ibid.*, p. 192.

TWENTY – FIVE

MR. NICE GUY

He was born on September 10, 1929 in Latrobe, Pennsylvania. We met for the first time in the 1940's when Arnold was in his teens before he left to go to college at Wake Forest. Here's how it happened.

Mr. Floyd Gerard was the Vice President of Kennemetal, Inc. of Latrobe, PA, America's premier producer of medium to large precision tungsten carbide products. Floyd was an avid golfer and one of my best friends. He and his wife Hildah, and their children would drive from Latrobe to Greensburg, PA, a relatively short distance, to attend church services. My wife, Ruth, and I and our young son, Roger were members of the same church. Dr. Allie Banker was the senior pastor of the church and the president of the Institute. I shared Floyd's obsession with golf.

Floyd also was a member of the Latrobe Country Club. His invitations for me to join him at the Club almost every Saturday from early Spring until late Fall were seldom turned down. We enjoyed the game and each other's company immensely. It was no secret that Latrobe Country Club is situated in one of western Pennsylvania's "garden spots."

The club professional and course superintendent (chief groundskeeper) was Arnold Palmer's father, Milford J. Palmer, better known by his nickname of "Deacon" Palmer. Deacon Palmer was associated with this fine golf club from 1921 until the time of his death in 1976. He had a great influence in Arnold's life and in the lives of many others.

By now you have guessed that "Mr. Nice Guy" is Arnold Palmer and for many good reasons. I call him Mr. Nice Guy, but Arnold Palmer is "larger than life" as a world-famous figure known to millions of people in numerous roles. He is known as the "King of Golf." For many years he led the largest non-uniformed "military organization" in history, *i.e., Arnie's Army*. In addition to being known as an internationally-famous golf "immortal," Arnold is a skilled pilot who flies a Cessna Citation VII Jet airplane to meet his golfing and business engagements.

Arnold Palmer is a highly-successful business executive who is President of the Arnold Palmer Enterprises, a wide-ranging and multiple-structured business and commercial venture. He owns the Latrobe Country Club where he caddied, helped his father, and first played golf. One of my greatest regrets is that I did not listen more closely to his advice when he was caddying for us and others in the "40ies." He also served as President and principal owner of the Bay Hill Club and Lodge in Orlando, Florida. He is a talented golf course designer who has his stamp on over 200 courses throughout the world.

As a victorious golfer, Arnold Palmer had won 92 championships in professional competition by the end of 1993. He won the Masters Championship four times (1958, 1960, 1962 and 1964), the British Open Championship (1961, 1962), and the United States Open Championship in 1960. On three occasions he finished second in the Professional Golfers Association Tournaments. Prior to these major golf accomplishments he won the U.S. Amateur Championship in 1954, several months before he turned a professional golfer and a "big" year for Arnold since this was the year he married Winifred ("Winnie") Walzer, his best friend and partner until her death occurred.

Arnold also served a three-year "hitch" in the U.S. Coast Guard. It would be nearly impossible to name the countless honors, awards, symbolic plaques, citations, and trophies Arnold Palmer has received already and, no doubt, with more to come. However, all that has been said about this outstanding man so far isn't why I think of him as "Mr. Nice Guy."

It is because he has been a devoted husband, a loving father to his two daughters, Peggy and Amy, and a kind and thoughtful grandfather to his grandchildren. It is because he was and is a humble person with a down-to-earth approach to people who surrounded him allowing him to be very accessible to others, a rare quality for someone who has achieved so much.

He began caddying at Latrobe Country Club in 1940 when he was eleven years old and was still willing to give caddy advice to amateur golfers such as Floyd Gerard and myself as he closed out his teen years. Arnold Palmer deserves the title "Mr. Nice Guy." What say you?

TWENTY – SIX

UP FOR GRABS

Werner Karl Heisenberg (1901-1976), German theoretical physicist, was a winner of the 1932 Nobel Prize for Physics at age 31. He was honored especially because of his discoveries in <u>ferromagnetism</u>, explained best in terms of the exchange of forces between electrons in neighboring atoms, and in his <u>uncertainty principle</u>, inherent in quantum mechanics which states "that at the microscopic level it is impossible to know both the momentum (p) and position (x) of a particle with absolute precision."[1] This same concept, often called the indeterminacy principle, applied to both energy and time as well with the same uncertainty.

The *principle of indeterminacy* is an apt description of the subject matter for this chapter since it deals with such issues as the lack of sureness, uncertainty, unpredictability, indecisiveness, ambivalence, insecurity, unstableness and other problematic approaches to life situations.

The term under consideration is *"up for grabs."* The British refer to the phrase *up for grabs* as an "Americanism."[2] It's a slang expression used when certain things are parceled out, or when issues are open and the options relating to them are allowable, or "up for grabs." A *grab bag* is a bag in which various things have been placed to be "grabbed," sight unseen, by a buyer

---

[1] Bothamley, Jennifer, *Dictionary of Theories*. London, England: Gale Research International, Ltd., 1993, p. 249.

[2] Rees, Paul S., *Don't Sleep Through the Revolution*. Waco, Texas: Word Books, 1969, p. 63.

who has paid a fixed price. What that person finds in the bag is "up for grabs." He or she is not sure what will be discovered within the bag until it is opened.

All of this is a long way from Dr. Heisenberg's recognition that when considering position and momentum, or energy and time, uncertainties in the measurements are produced. However, they do have something in common, and that is the *element of doubt*.

Like the ancient Roman god, the two-faced Janus (Jay-nus), god of gate and doors, of the beginnings and endings, for whom the month of January received its name, there appears the element of uncertainty. Strangely, *up for grabs* denotes both doubt (negative) and expectancy (positive).

In the positive thrust *up for grabs* offers something that is available, ready to be used. It is in the open and waiting to be grabbed by anyone who wants it. Tom Wicker, columnist for the *New York Times* newspaper and *The Nation* magazine, made a reference that appeared in an October 9, 2000 issue of *The Nation* regarding the concept under consideration. The headline of that article read: "Up For Grabs: The Supreme Court and the Election." In this case, both Al Gore and George W. Bush wanted to win the election desperately. Wicker described the scenario as "Up for Grabs."[3]

On the negative side there are references to wavering, vacillating, hesitating, fluctuating, questioning, doubting, to having mental reservations. Fear and degrees of apprehension are also factors involved.

The *Bible* does not commend *doubt*, especially as it relates to God and the Scriptures. It is the opposite of a quiet and steadfast confidence, an unwavering attitude that trusts God implicitly, and believes without vacillating in the promises He has made.

Elijah, the *Old Testament* prophet, while on Mount Carmel said to the multitude gathered there, "How long will you hesitate between two opinions?"[4] Joshua, Moses' successor, while giving his farewell address to the Israelites challenged them to set aside doubt and "choose for yourselves today whom you will serve."[5]

---

[3] Wicker, Tom, Article in *The Nation* magazine, October 9, 2000 issue.

[4] *Old Testament*, First Kings 18:21.

[5] *Ibid.*, Joshua 24:15.

100

Thomas, one of Jesus' disciples, was known for his doubting spirit. He would not believe that Jesus was resurrected from the dead. He said, "Unless I shall see in His hands the imprint of the nails, and put my finger into the place of the nails, and put my hand into His side, I will not believe."[6] When Jesus told him to do just that, Thomas confessed, "My Lord and my God!"[7] Jesus responded, "Because you have seen Me, have you believed? Blessed are they who did not see, and yet believed."[8]

The book of *James*, written by the half-brother of the Lord Jesus Christ, makes this dramatic statement, "But if any of you lacks wisdom, let him ask of God, who gives to all men generously and without reproach, and it will be given to him, But let him ask in faith without any doubting, for the one who doubts is like the surf of the sea driven and tossed by the wind. For let not that man expect that he will receive anything from the Lord, being a double-minded man, unstable in all his ways."[9]

When it's "Up for Grabs" take to heart the strong words of Jesus, "Have faith, doubt not."[10] These are His words of authority. What say you?

---

[6] *New Testament*, John 20:25.

[7] *Ibid.*, John 20:28.

[8] *Ibid.*, John 20:29.

[9] *Ibid.*, James 1:5-8.

[10] *Ibid.*, Matthew 21:21.

TWENTY – SEVEN

AMAZING GRACE

To those who lived around Cambridge, England in the 18th century he was known affectionately as the "Old Converted Sea Captain."

His identification can be confirmed in a small cemetery of a parish churchyard in Olney, England where the epitaph on a granite tombstone reads:

> John Newton, clerk, once an infidel and Libertine, a servant of slavers in Africa, was, by the rich mercy of our Lord and Savior Jesus Christ, preserved, restored, pardoned, and appointed to preach the Faith he had long labored to destroy.[1]

John Newton (1725-1807) went from a slave ship captain to become the highly respected pastor of Olney Church near Cambridge and later of Saint Mary Woolnoth Church in London. Before his death at age 82 he made this remarkable statement, "My memory is nearly gone, but I remember two things: that I am a great sinner and that Christ is a great Savior!"[2]

John Newton remembered these two remarkable experiential truths. We remember John Newton best for the following lines:

> Amazing grace- how sweet the sound- that saved a wretch like me! I once was lost but now am found, was blind but now I see.

---

[1] Osbeck, Kenneth W., *101 Hymn Stories*. Grand Rapids, MI: Kregel Publications, 1982, p. 28.
[2] *Ibid.*, p. 30.

'Twas grace that taught my heart to fear and grace my fears relieved; How precious did that grace appear-the hour I first believed!

Thru many dangers, toils and snares- I have already come; 'Tis grace hath brought me safe thus far, and grace will lead me home.

When we've been there ten thousand years, bright shining as the sun, We've no less days to sing God's praise than when we'd first begun.

These four stanzas of this most famous hymn have echoed for many decades in huge cathedrals with large pipe organs, in humble one-room rural church buildings with a worn-out, off-key piano accompaniment, on the playing fields before major sports events, in homes during family devotions, at grave sites in times of sorrow, on cruise ships plowing through ocean waves, in prison cells jam-packed with inmates, on mission fields in remote parts of the world, in government halls, in schools at every level, on buses carrying passengers to their destinations, and in many other venues. The lyrics are beautiful, singable, and the music is rich as an early American folk melody. The lines of these four famous stanzas have been memorized, perhaps more than any other hymn, by millions and millions of people from multiple nations encircling numerous cultures and transcending all races. Few people know, however, that John Newton got his inspiration from *First Chronicles 17:16 and 17*. And fewer still can quote from memory the three additional stanzas that John Newton wrote which did not appear in most hymn books. These verses read in this manner:

The Lord has promised good to me, His Word my hope secures; He will my shield and portion be as long as life endures.

Yes, when this heart and flesh shall fail, and mortal life shall cease, I shall possess within the veil, a life of joy and peace.

The earth shall soon dissolve like snow, the sun forbear to shine; But God, who called me here below, will be forever mine.[3]

What a tribute this grand old hymn is and has been! With each passing decade it seems to gain momentum in its popularity. And small wonder, as "Mr. Author Unknown" has written, "There is something about a fine old

---

[3] *Ibid.*, p. 31.

hymn that can stir the heart of a man; that can reach to the goal of his inmost soul as no mere preaching can."[4]

This is what an anonymous writer has said. What say you?

---

[4] *Ibid.*, Preface, p. xii.

TWENTY – EIGHT

LONELINESS

After encountering heavy anti-aircraft enemy fire power from a German embankment located a short distance north of Remagen, I was forced to crash land the burning Troop Carrier C-47 I was flying in a clearing on the west bank of the Rhine River. Even though we avoided the small arms fire on the ground, in just a matter of minutes my flight crew and I were captured by the Germans and force marched many kilometers to Stalag Luft 6-G.

Upon arrival at this German prisoner-of-war camp I learned that the majority of prisoners were Russian. There were French and Italian prisoners there also. My crew, made up of my co-pilot, my radio operator, and my crew chief, and myself were informed that our presence swelled the ranks of American prisoners to a total of 182.

Initially, I was placed in solitary confinement for the purpose of intensive interrogation. Under Geneva regulations for warfare all that I was responsible to give my captors was my name, rank and my serial number. They wanted more, much more, but I refused adamantly to give it to them. While in solitary confinement, after such traumatic experiences, I found for the first time that I could remember a serious attack of in-depth *loneliness*. Thanks to a strong awareness of God's presence and His power to act, it was temporary. Yet, it was devastating while it lasted.

Loneliness is a universal malady. It is no respecter of persons. It is a common occurrence for many. Marvin J. Rosenthal claims that "Loneliness is a tragic thing to experience. Ask the woman that does her shopping at four food stores, buying a few items at each stop so she can chat for a moment with the clerk. Ask the old man whose wife is deceased and children live in faraway places, as he stares listlessly out the window. Ask the teenager whose parents are too busy to give time or show affection."[1]

Dr. Gary Collins speaks of the loneliness of students at an impersonal campus.[2] He mentions that there is loneliness for those in the armed services.[3] There is loneliness for the single adult who has difficulty finding acceptance in the community where he or she lives.[4] He recognizes that some young adults are often critical of older people and don't want to have them around, which increases loneliness for "senior citizens."[5] Persons who have lost loved ones through death, Collins points out, often have to learn to live with overwhelming loneliness.[6] Examples of causes for loneliness seem endless and the effects can be devastating if the loneliness persists and grows in intensity.

Philip Yancey and Tim Stafford want to know if loneliness is a "cruel trick to keep us mired in self-pity?"[7] Even more critical than self-pity is the bottom-line conclusion reached by psychologist David Claerbaut who bluntly writes, "Simply stated: People can get sick from feeling lonely; and if the feeling is severe enough, they can die from it."[8]

Because of its seriousness, *loneliness* does need a remedy. It needs to be overcome and there are professional helps, caring groups, and practical guidelines that can be found and utilized. To seek such means requires an "admission of loneliness" and this open recognition does not come easily since to do so makes one feel vulnerable and stigmatized, and often leads to

---

[1] Rosenthal, Marvin J., *Not Without Design*. West Collingswood, New Jersey: The Friends of Israel Gospel Ministry, Inc., 1980, p. 49.

[2] Collins, Gary R., *Man In Transition*. Carol Stream, Illinois: Creation House, 1971, p. 106.

[3] *Ibid.*, p. 111.

[4] *Ibid.*, p. 121.

[5] *Ibid.*, p. 140.

[6] *Ibid.*, p. 143.

[7] Yancey, Philip and Stafford, Tim, *Unhappy Secrets of the Christian Life*. Grand Rapids, MI: Zondervan Publishing House, 1979, p. 62.

[8] Claerbaut, David, *Liberation From Loneliness*. Wheaton, Illinois: Tyndale House Publishers, Inc., 1984, p. 36.

further isolation since most people do not want to be around someone who is lonely. They do not like the negative and depressing vibes.

Before "wrapping up" these few observations about *loneliness*, let me differentiate between *loneliness*, both in space and spirit, and *solitude*, often a welcome relief from too many social contacts and psychological pressures. David Claerbaut makes a distinction that "being alone is not synonymous with being lonely."[9] In fact, to him, solitude "is so different from loneliness that it can actually help defeat loneliness."[10] Yancey and Stafford concur as they admit, "Loneliness is not the same as aloneness."[11]

Solitude offers opportunities to blot out daily concerns, gives us a time to integrate, to reflect, to pray, to praise. Just as solitude nourished and rebuilt Christ's spirit as He quietly was alone with the Heavenly Father in prayer, it can be a wonderful help to us. This is what I believe regarding loneliness and solitude. What say you?

[9] *Ibid.*, p. 11.
[10] *Ibid.*
[11] Yancey and Stafford, *op. cit.*, p. 63.

TWENTY – NINE

RESULTS

Try this formula for getting results: *Motivations* times *Abilities* times *Opportunities* equals *Achievements*.

Take it by steps in proper sequence. A person who is strongly motivated, but lacks ability to do the task, even when given opportunities, will be a mediocre achiever. The reason is obvious. That person does not have the abilities necessary to achieve. Or, a person who lacks motivation, even though greatly gifted with skills and abilities and given adequate opportunity, will be a mediocre achiever. The deficiency is motivation. Finally, a person with excellent motivation and tremendous ability will go nowhere unless he or she is given opportunity, or can make those opportunities occur.

There is another factor in this formula that should not be overlooked. It was <u>times</u>, not <u>plus</u>. *Times* is *multiplication* while *plus* is *addition*. Multiplication consists of many parts, and has a cumulative effect allowing for complex diversity within the formula development. Addition, on the other hand, even though leading to an increase in desired effect is more limited in scope. Consequently, optimum achievement gives exponential results when multiplication is the process.

A computer specialist would say let's find a search engine that can supply us with some excellent achievers who have strong motivations, specialized abilities, and who either were given or made opportunities to achieve in outstanding ways. In other words, it is *passion, performance, and potential multiplied.*

Some great achievers include Martin Luther who nailed his convictions on a door and made an amazing difference in the religious world; Lee Iacocca who came from the outside to reinvent the structure of Chrysler Corporation from the top down; Martin Luther King, Jr. who had a dream he was willing to die for and as a result played a major role in changing society in America; the Apostle Paul who was converted from destroyer to deliverer and became God's agent of biblical truth and word evangelism; William Carey who went from what his friends regarded as a miserable hack to become a missionary hero.

Many have heard of Chuck Colson who was transformed from a political prisoner to a profitable prophet to bring promise to thousands of condemned convicts; Stephen Jobs whose radical concepts brought a mighty corporation to humiliation and despair; Henry Ford who revolutionized the automobile industry; Thomas Edison, regarded as an eccentric failure, who became one of the greatest inventors of all time.

Fewer, perhaps, have heard of Chester Colson who went from laughing-stock to the inventor of the Xerox process. Bill Gothard, even though a single person, did more for frustrated parents rearing difficult children during the last half of the 20th century than almost anyone else. There was also Robert Millikan, Nobel Prize winner in physics, who tapped into the power of the atom; Walt Disney who introduced gigantic strides in the world of animation and theme parks; Carla Maria Giulini, when conductor of the Los Angeles Philharmonic, made the world realize that the great mystery of music-making requires real friendship among those who work together; Andrew Carnegie, world renown Scottish industrialist in America, who taught the world how to use his wealth to benefit others; Charles Schultz who made Snoopy top dog while using his comic strips to teach the world great moral philosophies of life; and Alexander Graham Bell who electrified the world with his invention of the telephone. All of these are merely the "tip of the iceberg" when it comes to outstanding achievements.[1]

---

[1] Some of these examples emerged from reading the book, *The Top Ten Mistakes Leaders Make* which was written by Hans Finzel (Colorado Springs, CO: Cook Communication Ministries, 1994.) Other examples came from many resources out of my library.

The common denominators were motivations, abilities, and opportunities. A significant aspect of the last component is how large was the proportion of those who "made" the opportunities come to life over those who grasped the opportunities that came to them. That's the challenge for researchers.

Most of us are familiar with *Parkinson's Law* which states: "Work expands to fill the time available for its completion."[2] Perhaps it is time *now* to expand our efforts for greater achievement by examining the motivations, the abilities, and the opportunities that are available to us. What say you?

---

[2] Bothamley, Jennifer, *Dictionary of Theories*. London: Gale Research International, Ltd., 1993, p. 399.

THIRTY

NAMES

George Whillikens from the city of High Point in North Carolina was a real person. He was known as a gentlemanly scholar who had a pet peeve. He despaired deeply about swearing and denounced it vigorously. To combat this "ugly demeanor" he advocated the use of milder euphemisms by those who had the tendency to swear. He suggested that habitual swearers should substitute such expressions as "ding-bust-it," "doggone," "dag-nab-it," and so forth in place of swear words. As a result of his concentrated effort many people began to use his name as a euphemism for swearing. Thus, "G. Whillikens" was born into our vocabulary.

Language matters and names are important! There was a time when my wife, Ruth, and I and our daughter, Ginger, were riding on a train from London, England to visit our son, Roger, who was studying at the University in Edinburgh, Scotland. En route one of the passengers, a resident of Edinburgh, shared a "Scottish story" with us. He asked if we had heard of the famous Scottish poet, Mr. Robert Burns. Of course, our response was affirmative. He said that Mr. Burns was so respected by his people that no one wished to offend by referring to him as "Bobby Burns" or "Bob Burns." Instead he was known as Robert Burns or Mr. Burns. Our passenger friend then asked a question, "After all, would you refer to your New Testament personality as 'Jack, the Baptist'?" We agreed he had a point well-taken. He smiled. It was sort of a smile of victory.

The late Sir Winston Churchill described one of his most vocal opponents by observing that he had a genius for compressing a minimum of thought into a maximum of words. On one occasion, this "friend" of Sir Winston Churchill patted the British Prime Minister on his "protruding tummy" and asked, "What is it going to be—a boy or a girl?" Without a moment of hesitation, Mr. Churchill replied, "If it is a boy, I will name it after the king. If it is a girl, I will name it after the queen. But, if it is just wind, I will name it after you."

The naming of Quisling of Norway is equated with treason and disloyalty. Vidkun Quisling (1887-1945) was a Norwegian politician who betrayed his country to the German Nazis and is forever known as a traitor. To the Dutch people of the Netherlands, the name of *Zondervan* means "without a last name." Jonathan *Wainwright* was a wagon maker. Bill *Cooper* was a barrel maker.

The name of *Roy Riegals* carries with it "running in the wrong direction." How did this happen? It occurred in Pasadena, California on January 1, 1929. The University of California football team was playing against Georgia Tech in the Rose Bowl game. Both teams were evenly matched and it was a hard fought game throughout.

Just before halftime California was on Tech's 20-yard line and was moving the ball with momentum. When California's center snapped the football, the quarterback fumbled the ball and it rolled to the 38-yard line. Roy Riegals, a Cal player, saw the loose ball, grabbed it quickly, and started to run as fast as he could—in the wrong direction! He was finally tackled from behind by one of his own teammates on the California two-yard line. On the next play, Georgia Tech pushed the California team backward and tackled their halfback in the end zone for a safety giving them two points. The final score of the game was Georgia Tech 8 and California 7. The University of California lost the game by one point due to Roy Riegals' "gift."

The emphasis by Saint Luke in the *Book of Acts*, Chapters 3 and 4, is on the *name* of the Lord Jesus Christ.[1] The Apostle Paul said that the name of Jesus Christ is "above every name."[2]

---

[1] *New Testament of the Bible*, Acts 3:6, 16; 4:7, 10, 12, 17, 18, 30.
[2] *Ibid.*, Philippians 2:9-11.

Jesus Christ called Himself by many different descriptive names. He was also called by various names by others in the Bible. For example, among them He was known as *The Way* (John 14:6), *The Truth* (John 14:6), *The Life* (John 14:6), *The Good Shepherd* (John 10:11), *The Light* (John 1:7), *The Resurrection* (John 11:25), *The Son of Man* (Mark 2:28), *The Prince of Peace* (Isaiah 9:6), *The Bread of Life* (John 6:35), *Immanuel* (Isaiah 7:14), *The Word* (John 1:1), *The Savior* (Second Peter 3:18), *The Mighty God* (Isaiah 9:6), *The Wonderful Counselor* (Isaiah 9:6), *The Everlasting Father* (Isaiah 9:6), *The Son of God* (First John 4:15), *The Lord* (Matthew 8:8), *God* (John 20:28). His names had real purposes. For instance, the Bible indicates that an angel told Joseph, "You shall call His name Jesus, for it is He who will save his people from their sins."[3]

"A name," as Warren W. Wiersbe states, "implies much more than identification; it carries with it authority, reputation, and power."[4] This is especially true with Biblical names.

Lawrence O. Richards confirms Wiersbe's observations when he writes, "In biblical cultures a name did more than identify; it communicated something of the essence, the character, or the reputation of the person or thing named."[5]

Shakespeare asks, "What is in a name?"[6] He answers, "That which we call a rose, by any other name would smell as sweet."[7] He also acknowledges, "Who steals my purse steals trash; but he that filches from me my good name, robs me of that which not enriches him, and makes me poor indeed."[8]

Names are very important! Thomas Fuller (1608-1661), and English clergyman, said, "A name is a kind of face whereby one is known."[9] What say you?

---

[3] *New Testament*, Matthew 1:21.

[4] Wiersbe, Warren W., *Be Dynamic*. Colorado Springs, Colorado: Chariot Victor Publishing, 1987, p. 35.

[5] Richards, Lawrence O., *Expository Dictionary of Bible Words*. Grand Rapids, Michigan: Zondervan Publishing House, 1985, p. 453.

[6] Shakespeare in *The New Dictionary of Thoughts*. Standard Book Company, 1957, p. 454.

[7] *Ibid.*

[8] *Ibid.*

[9] Fuller, Thomas, *The New Dictionary of Thoughts*, op. cit., p. 433.

THIRTY - ONE

PURPOSES

He was my friend and we enjoyed good times together, especially when ministering to students at Hampden DuBose Academy in Zellwood, Florida. I refer to the late Richard DeHaan, at that time the President of Radio Bible Class Ministries with headquarters in Grand Rapids, Michigan.

Richard liked to tell the story of the cowboy who made application for an insurance policy. When the insurance agent asked the cowboy if he had ever had any serious accidents, the cowboy replied, "Nope, but a horse kicked in two of my ribs once, and a rattlesnake did bite me on my leg." The agent followed up on these admissions by asking, "Wouldn't you call these accidents?" The answer came, "Naw, they did these things on purpose!"

The word *purpose* comes from the French and Latin languages and carried with it the meaning of placing before, of intending, of resolving, of planning. It refers to *design*, not something that happens accidentally. To be *purposeful* is to aim resolutely at a specific goal.

When you tap into the Greek word *prothesis* and *boule*, you see God's sovereignty in action denoting a decision that had been made, and in the case of the latter of the two words, a fixed intention that is in order. This differs from a human intention or plan that may or may not be achieved.

From this perspective, dealing with God's great ability to motivate and move men and women who catch the vision of God's presence, power, and purposes, Rick Warren, the founding pastor of Saddleback Church in Lake Forest, California, has opened much more than a Pandora's box in starting an explosion of focused attention on achieving meaningful purpose in every area of life. The results of his insights and common-sense principles, biblically -sound and action-oriented, have revolutionized not only Christians and the churches they attend but many non-Christians in our secular society as well. It has been and continues to be a modern and universal phenomenon.

The secret of his success is that it is no secret! Rather, it is downright dependence upon the Holy Spirit of God to bring purpose to living and more than adequate spiritual resources to meet human needs. Who among us can predict the fall-out of these bombshells of truth for purposeful holy living? It is exciting to watch the process and to evaluate the progress.

Pastor Warren makes the promise that by the time the readers firmly grasp God's purpose for their lives, they will see the "big picture" of how all the pieces fit together. The promise is being realized in the lives of hundreds of thousands, if not millions of people who read or have contact with his messages.

The process may become complex but the key is simple. It all has to do with *purpose*, God's purpose for our lives. Warren stresses that we were born *by his purpose* and *for his purpose*.[1] It's as the cowboy said in Richard DeHaan's illustration. There is nothing accidental about any of it!

Richard Leider, a man who experienced hardships and setbacks in his own life, wrote a penetrating book dealing with life's purposes. He asked questions about having a clear picture of where a person is going and being satisfied with the targets or goals to get there. He wanted to know what methods were in place to track progress and what values were important in life. It would help the reader greatly to get acquainted with the profound materials found in Leider's *The Power of Purpose*.[2]

Achieving *purpose in life* requires the development of logical, specific, conceivable, achievable, believable, measurable, and desirable goals. To reach these goals, Ron Jenson, who is an internationally known author and an

---

[1] Warren, Rick, *The Purpose Driven Life*. Grand Rapids, Michigan: Zondervan, 2002, p. 9.
[2] Leider, Richard, *The Power of Purpose*. New York, NY: Fawcett Gold Medal, 1985.

executive consultant, suggests four necessary skills: 1) See your purpose clearly. Know where you are going; 2) Want your purpose desperately. This deals with motivation; 3) Accomplish your purpose wholeheartedly. For this total commitment is needed; and, 4) Follow your purpose faithfully. This requires endurances. Don't quit.[3]

I listened intently in a packed auditorium at Georgia State University in Atlanta in the 1960's to the things that Dr. Victor Frankl, a world-renown psychiatrist, was saying. He emphasized how absolutely essential it was for those in the German concentration camp with him to retain a *realistic sense of meaning, a purpose for which to live* in order to survive. For anyone desiring to know more about Dr. Frankl's experiences, you can read his book, *Man's Search For Meaning: An Introduction to Logotherapy*, found in most sizable libraries.[4]

In these brief paragraphs you have learned from Richard DeHaan, Rick Warren, Richard Leider , Ron Jenson and Victor Frankl concerning the value of a purpose-centered life. The question now is "What say you?"

---

[3] Jenson, Ron, *Make A Life, Not Just A Living.* Nashville, TN: Thomas Nelson Publishers, 1995, pp. 84-87.

[4] Frankl, Victor, *Man' Search For Meaning: An Introduction to Logotherapy.* Boston, MS: Beacon Press, 1962.

THIRTY - TWO

CORPORATE LANDLORDS

Hardy Green, an Associate Editor of *Business Week* magazine would describe the comparatively small city located in the southern tier of New York State where I grew up as a child as "a town named for its corporate landlord." My birthplace was Corning, New York, and the "corporate landlord" that Mr. Green referred to is the Corning Glass Works, now known as Corning, Inc.

Mr. Green's editorial, "A Real-Life Willy Wonka," included Alcoa, Tennessee; Kohler, Wisconsin; Kennecott, Alaska; and Hershey, Pennsylvania as towns with a similar affinity toward corporate landlords.[1]

Corning was named for Erastus Corning who, as a railroad executive and financial investor from Albany, New York, helped get this community established as a village during the 1830's. It remained a village until incorporated as a city in 1890. Initially, Corning got it's reputation for being the focal point for shipping coal, lumber, and farm products to other locations. Things changed drastically in 1868, shortly after the Civil War ended.

In June of 1868 a foundation was laid in Corning for a new glass plant. Instigator for this historic event was Elias B. Hungerford of Corning. He had patented a glass window blind and was responsible for urging the wealthy Houghton family and its partners to move the Brooklyn Flint Glass Works to Corning. Houghtons agreed to this arrangement providing another firm

---

[1] Green, Hardy, "A Real-Life Willy Wonka," *Business Week*, January 23, 2006, p. 92.

123

that made cut glass, known as Hoare & Daily, would join with them. The agreement was made. The foundation for the new plant was laid in June of 1868 and a new era in Corning began. Operations began on October 22, 1868.

Corning's population exploded as a large migration from Brooklyn and Long Island took place. A local building boom occurred. Suddenly, Corning, New York developed into a glass manufacturing village. The Industrial Revolution of that era had arrived in the southern tier location. It was now "on the map."

Growth continued as the Rand Drill Company of nearby Painted Post, NY joined forces with the Ingersoll-Sergeant Drill Company and the large plant of Ingersoll-Rand became one of the largest manufacturers of rock drills and compressors. Next came the establishment of the Corning Brick Works in 1878, which later became known as the Corning Terra Cotta and Supply Company. Within two decades this formerly quiet community located at a confluence of railroads and split by the Chemung River which overflowed its banks often in the Spring, became a place to gain world-wide attention.

However, notwithstanding the development of Ingersoll-Rand and the Corning Terra Cotta and Supply Company, Corning was to build its reputation on the Corning Glass Works and its chief landlords, the Houghton family.

The names of Amory Houghton, Sr. (1812-1882), Alanson Bigelow Houghton (1863-1941), Amory Houghton (1899-1981), Amory Houghton, Jr., also known as Amo Houghton (1926-), and James R. Houghton, ("Jamie", who retired as Chairman of the Board in 1996, only to return in 2001 in order to "save" the company from financial disaster, are "big names" in this corporate landlord city. Corning has given to the Houghtons a mythic status because of their generations of public service, political expertise, philanthropy and civic service. Alanson was the first U.S. ambassador to Germany after World War I. Amory, Sr., his son was President Ike Eisenhower's ambassador to France. Amo Houghton has been a Republican member of the U.S. Congress since 1987. Even though the Houghtons' investment in Corning, Inc, is down about 5%, its reputation as "Corning's landlord" remains solid.

Whereas such companies as Ford, Wal-Mart and Cargill are known for their size and Japan's Kongo Gumi Company is celebrated for its more than 1,400 years of existence, the former Corning Glass Works, makers of Pyrex and Silex wares, and many other technical glassware products such as light bulbs, television tubes, Corning cookware, ceramic substrates, optical fiber, crystal displays and more, is best known for its corporate landlords, the Houghton family with their mansion residence on a sprawling 115-acre estate. Only time will tell how significant was the landlord impact on Corning, New York.

Even though Corning, Inc. is a long way from its peak employment of 46,000 worldwide, and its market value of $100 billion as a high-tech star, it is still a force to be reckoned with; and even though the city of Corning is "not what it used to be" with a census figure of only 10,842 in 2000, it deserves a visit for numerous reasons. Chief among them is the unique Corning Museum of Glass on the north-side, which contains the world's most comprehensive collection of glass objects from ancient times to the present. You can also enjoy a visit to the Rockwell Museum of Western and Native Art with its many paintings and sculptures. In fact, Corning, New York, our corporate landlord city, has been cited on numerous occasions as "one of the top art destinations in the United States" by *American Style* readers.

You will not get a free Hershey bar in Corning. You will have to go to the corporate landlord city of Hershey, Pennsylvania for that. But, you can get a wonderful keepsake from one of the glass firms there, even personally make you own glass souvenir. I think that you will be glad that you did. What say you?

THIRTY - THREE

DREAM

Dial back to the year 1940. That is when Leigh Harline composed the music and Ned Washington wrote the lyric for the song, *When You Wish Upon a Star*. This musical number, taken from the Disney film *Pinocchio*, promised that "If your heart is in a dream, no request is too extreme, when you wish upon a star as dreamers do."

It was the famous Irving Berlin who, in 1942, had the world singing, "I'm dreaming of a white Christmas, just like the ones I used to know." We keep on singing this year after year.

Fantasy took another step forward in 1945 when Richard Rodgers and Oscar Hammerstein II collaborated on a song that included these lines, "I keep wishing I were someone else, walking down a strange new street and hearing the words that I've never heard from a girl I've yet to meet. I'm as busy as a spider spinning daydreams, spinning spinning daydreams. I'm as giddy as a baby on a swing."

Dreams, daydreams, what do they all mean? Semanticists think of dreams as a series of mental images during a person's sleep, or an ambition, an aspiration. They label "daydreaming" as imaginative thoughts that occur while we are wide-awake, or as a state of mind which is characterized by both abstraction and a flight from reality. A "pipe dream" may be a vain hope of a fantastic nature. Such terms as woolgathering or stargazing may enter into the mix.

Dreams should be taken seriously. All, or most all, of us dream from time to time. Some of these dreams are nice and some are ugly. Forecasts based on dreams are called "oneiromancy." Interpretation of dreams is known as "oneirology" and one who interprets dreams is referred to as an "oneirocritic."

Martin Luther King, Jr. gave a memorable "I Have A Dream" speech in which he set forth a desirable goal of justice and equality based on human dignity, not skin color. His profound thoughts are echoed frequently.

Joseph of Old Testament renown was a dreamer par excellent. He got into serious trouble when he told his siblings and his parents about two of his dreams which were suggestive of potential future greatness on his part, along with his brothers subservience to him. Later, while imprisoned for a crime he did not commit, Joseph interpreted two dreams, one for Pharaoh's chief butler and another for his chief baker. Both dreams came true. Two years later Joseph was called upon to interpret two dreams that the Pharaoh had which none of his wise men could interpret. In doing so, Joseph found favor with the ruler of Egypt and was promoted to become Pharaoh's Prime Minister, second in rank to Pharaoh himself.

In the *Bible* we also learn about Daniel, an Old Testament prophet, who was given by God the spiritual gift of visions and interpreting dreams (*Daniel 1:17*). When Nebuchadnezzar, the king of Babylon, asked the seemingly impossible: i.e., the interpretation of his undisclosed dream, God honored Daniel by revealing both the dream of a fourfold image referring to four world empires, and the impact this would have preparing for God's Messianic kingdom (*Daniel 2:44*). For this, Daniel was made Prime Minister of the Babylonian kingdom. Later, Daniel interpreted the king's dream of a fallen tree (*Daniel 4:18-37*).

Think about some of the dreams you have had. Perhaps you have been asked by others to interpret their dreams. One thing is for certain, dreams may focus on a world of unreality but, nevertheless, dreams are a realistic part of our lives.

Do you believe that God could reveal His will in dreams today just as He did centuries ago? Would it be necessary for Him to do so given that we have the Word of God (*The Bible*) and the Holy Spirit to guide us? Remember that the angel of the Lord did speak to Joseph in a dream (*Matthew 1:20-24*). With these thoughts in mind, what say you?

THIRTY - FOUR

REPETITION

The quotation, "Those who cannot remember the past are condemned to repeat it," did not come from the *Bible*. It is, in fact, a statement made by George Santayana. Mr. Santayana was born in 1863 while the Civil War was in progress in the United States. During his lifetime he lived for a time in the United States, even though he was born in Spain and spent most of his life in his native country. His full name was Jorge Augustin Nicolas Ruiz de Santayana. From 1907 until 1912 he taught as a professor on the Harvard University faculty. George Santayana died in 1952.

Those scholars who think of Mr. Santayana as a philosopher who wrote the five-volume tome, *The Life of Reason* in 1905 and 1906, and *Realms of Being* beginning in 1927, seldom recall that he began his professional career as a poet.

Santayana's quotation is intended to place the spotlight on the subject of *repetition*. Repetition takes place when that which is said, made, done, or happens again, or again and again, occurs. It may happen to a student who has to take over a course he or she has failed to pass. It may refer to a person who has been convicted a number of times for criminal activity or violating the law. It may reference a rebroadcast of a radio or television program. This list of repetitive instances could continue *ad infinitum*. When repetition occurs over and over it is often called *reiteration*.

I learned a great lesson about *repetition*. The situation took place in Altoona, Pennsylvania. The year was 1946 and the setting was early winter. Altoona was, and still is, one of several locations that sponsored a satellite facility as an off-main-campus Pennsylvania State University, then known as Pennsylvania State College.

I was a student in the Freshman class enjoying an easy commute from our home in El Dorado, a suburb of Altoona, Pennsylvania. I was also enjoying the benefits of a photographic memory. The various classes seemed easy, at times boring. I was riding along on a straight A average when a "flu bug" invaded our home. For one week I was confined to bed rest. Unfortunately, the flu was not the only malady causing suffering and discomfort. I was also afflicted with the subtle disease of over-confidence, otherwise known as pride. *Pride* is the only sickness known to mankind that makes almost everyone else ill except for the one who has it.

Upon returning to class I did not ask anyone what I had missed, determined to "go with the flow" as if I had never been absent. The flu was gone but not the pride!

My philosophy class was more exciting than the others for two reasons. It was taught by an exceptional scholar by the name of Dr. Edwin Zoller. Secondly, he has a goatee which moved majestically when he spoke and, since he was an artist as well, he illustrated his teaching with unusual drawings on the blackboard. One I remember especially was his drawing of an old-fashioned desk that had many "openings" beneath its roll-top. He warned us against "pigeon-holing" each class we took at college, with the admonition that we should integrate them into an understandable, meaningful whole.

When the time arrived for the mid-term examination in his class, Dr. Zoller circulated a five question test with each answer evaluated at twenty points. I read quickly the entire exam and was stunned as I saw the inquiry found in the second question. It asked for a full explanation of *philosophical eclecticism*. Obviously, this subject matter had been presented and discussed while I was ill with the flu. The term was new and unknown to me. I raised my hand and when Dr. Zoller came to my desk I asked, "Is this term spelled correctly?" He smiled, hesitated a moment, and then replied, "Yes, it is. You may be in trouble. Correct?"

The truth of the matter was that I was in serious trouble with an automatic loss of twenty points, and we both knew it! I finished question one with ease. When I arrived at the second question I wrote, "Please see the answer to this question at the end of the examination paper." What a stupid thing to write. I guess that this "stall" was designed in hopes that I would receive a special revelation from God.

After completing the four answers to the other questions I looked at my watch. I still had fifteen minutes available to give an answer to question number two, even though I still did not understand the term.

I began to write, noting what I could about metaphysics, ethics, logic, morality, epistemology, and aesthetics (actually not a bad approach to eclecticism I later discovered). In my desperation I filled two and one-half pages of rambling philosophy. As I handed the exam booklet to Dr. Zoller the thought did cross my mind that perhaps he would give me some credit for effort.

When the examination paper was returned, Dr. Zoller wrote these words, "Mr. Williams, as I understand it you are planning for a career in Christian ministry. When you have time, please refer to *Matthew 6:7* and in place of the word *praying* substitute the word *writing*."

Hurriedly, I did so, and read, "And when you are writing, do not use meaningless repetition, as the Gentiles so, for they suppose that they will be heard for their many words." To this Dr. Zoller added, "Minus twenty."

What a great, though hard, lesson in honesty regarding *repetition*. Medication and bed rest cured the flu. Dr. Zoller gave the right dose of medication for a bad case of pride and being unprepared. At least, those are my thoughts and convictions. Now, what say you?

THIRTY - FIVE

MELODY

During my four score plus years I have quoted gifted physician Oliver Wendell Holmes, Sr., and his venerable son, jurist and Supreme Court Justice Oliver Wendell Holmes, Jr., many times. It is most appropriate, therefore, that the final chapter of this book *What Say You?* Would end with a quotation for the senior member of this highly respected family.

Physician Holmes wrote these lines in 1853. They appeared in *The Voiceless* and were recorded as follows:

> A few can touch the magic string,
>   And noisy Fame is proud to win them:
> Alas for those that never sing,
>   But die with all their music in them![1]

The last line, frequently expressed, was boxing champion Gene Tunney's favorite quotation. So that I may not die with all the music yet in me, I close the chapters of this book with some thoughts on the simple theme, "Melody."

I finished high school by the time the big band era was getting underway with a multitude of bands and gifted vocalists. I almost wrote "in full swing"

---

[1] Carruth, Gorton and Ehrlich, Eugene, *American Quotations*. New York: Portland House, 1988, p. 391.

and perhaps that would have been appropriate for the time when each band was trying to develop its own style, its particular and unique *sound*.

Orchestra leaders that had achieved prominence in the late 30's and early 40's included: Benny Goodman, Glenn Miller, Tommy and Jimmy Dorsey, Vaughn Monroe, Louie Primo, Tiny Thornhill, Kaye Kyser, Henry Mancini, Mantovani, Percy Faith, Guy Lombardo, Hugo Winterhalter, Nelson Riddle, Ray Anthony, Les Baxter, Artie Shaw, Gene Krupa, Freddy Martin, Ray Bloch, Glen Grey, Harry James, David Rose, Les Paul, Sammy Kaye, Frankie Laine, Les Brown, Paul Whiteman, Louis Armstrong, Duke Ellington, Dizzy Gillespie, Lionel Hampton, Dave Brubeck, Eddie Duchin, Ted Weems, Hal Kemp, Jan Garber, Xavier Cugart, Carmen Cavallaro, Count Basie, Erroll Garner, Woody Herman, Alvino Ray and many more.

It was a known fact in our household that I annoyed my parents as I sat beside the radio and "pounded out the beat." I bought dozens of big band records, sang the lyrics along with the vocalist, followed them to the musical casinos, and dreamed of the day I would form my own band, "Willie Williams and his Syncopating Serenaders of Sweet and Swanky Swing." Those were the days!

With a voice that even a loving mother would not commend, I sang the words of numerous tunes, such as: *Moonlight Serenade, Lazy River, Bei Mir Bist Du Schoen, Goodnight Irene, On Top of Old Smokey, If I Didn't Care, I Don't Want To Set The World On Fire, To Each His Own, I've Got a Girl in Kalamazoo, Three Coins in a Fountain, Mairzy Doats, That's Amore, Pennsylvania 6-5000*, and many more. There's one song that I sang over and over again. Part of the lyrics went, "The song has ended, but the melody lingers on."

As you may have guessed, that is my convenient way to segue into the *melody* of this book which requires only three words to identify it,

What Say You?

The *melody* of any song is designed to command our attention. Technically, it is a series of measured and accented tones meant to inspire and produce imaginative creativity. This book has presented a series of measured and accented ideas meant to inspire you to think, and to cause you to supplement the necessary *harmony* to support the *melody* and to blend into a *rhythm* that will make the subject matter timely and timeless in your personal experience.

I hope it can become "*mission accomplished.*" *What say you?*

GLOSSARY

Amazing Grace – What a tribute this grand old hymn is and has been! With each passing decade it seems to gain momentum in its popularity. And small wonder, as "Mr. Author Unknown" has written, "There is something about a fine old hymn that can stir the heart of a man; that can reach to the goal of his inmost soul as no mere preaching can." Discover in this chapter three verses practically unknown that John Newton penned.

As If – The German philosopher Hans Vashinger, who was born in 1852 and died in 1933, made the expression "As If" into a philosophy or a hypothesis in the year 1911. His intention in doing so was to describe how thinking and acting proceeded by unproven or contradictory assumptions which were treated *by faith as if* they were true beyond reasonable doubt. We know today the value of faith in dealing with many of life's assumptions, and we know also that "Without faith it is impossible to please God" *(Hebrews 11:6)*.

Assumptions – This word is used to describe the tendency to take too much for granted. It can mean acting presumptuously or suppositionally without concrete supporting evidence to do so.

Balance – Balance suggests the offsetting or contrasting of parts so as to produce an aesthetic equilibrium in the whole. The word has a relation to weights and measures where scales indicate an evenness. It also refers to a lifestyle that avoids extremes. It is symmetry in motion.

Boomerang – Literally, it is an aerodynamically shaped throwing instrument used basically for sports activities where a return to the thrower is anticipated with accurate precision. Symbolically, it indicates that when the motive for giving is selfless and generous it will bring return dividends. It is also used often for decorative purposes.

Calling An Audible – This football term relates to the obvious reality of change, the necessity of doing so, and what is often the pressure associated with dealing with change. Indirectly, it allows for the realization that the change may fail, cause a degree of confusion, and make matters even worse. However, the intent us is to bring a more successful result than the one previously planned when discovery was made of its potential for failure. The "play" to be made at the line in a football game differs from the one planned by the team in the huddle. Thus, the quarterback calls an "audible" to change the prearranged play while waiting for the snap from the center to start the team moving.

Catch—22 – This unique term refers to a paradox in a law, a regulation, or a practice that is illogical and makes one a victim of its provisions, no matter what attempts are made to change the situation. It leads to a frustrating and confusing condition in which one is trapped by contradictory components. It is generally thought of as a "no-win" situation. This unusual term was coined by Joseph Heller in a novel he wrote in 1961.

Corporate Landlords – When a town or city is named after its corporate landlords, that place takes on somewhat of a "utopian complex." Some people refer to these places, like Hershey, Pennsylvania; Corning, New York; Kennecott, Alaska; Alcoa, Tennessee; and Kohler, Wisconsin as "philanthropic dictatorships that blend together commerce with good works and civic pride."

Couch Potato – This is a slang expression to describe a very lazy person who sits or reclines much more than what is normal. It is lethargy personified when there is no physical necessity for doing so. Needless to add, the British potato farmers do not appreciate the references to the word *potato*. I suspect that manufactures of *couches* might have strong feelings about this slang expression also.

Dream – Dreams are series of mental images during a person's sleep. They may also represent an ambition or an aspiration. Daydreams refer to imaginative thoughts that occur while we are wide-awake. They may be classified, also, as states of mind which are characterized by both abstractions and a flight from reality.

Heartaches – These are strong emotional reactions to difficult circumstances that create sorrow and disappointment. They may greatly affect the person's behavior and could, in some cases, injure relationships.

If Only – This conjecture has its roots in the expectations of *hope*. It can be unrealistic or realistic expectations. Either way, hope is the chief component since the expression, "if only," points to a desire for something different from that which is.

Interruptions – Interruptions can be positive or negative. From a positive perspective they can lead to rest, promising results, or pleasant surprises. Negatively, they can be intrusive, an invasion of privacy, a threat to an important on-going activity, or a stinging irritation. Either way, our attitudinal and behavior patters are affected by them.

Letter – High – This expression, borrowed from the game of baseball, is a standard for flexible measurement and interpretative understanding in the dynamic process of communication. Its variations point concretely to the fact that communication is *not* an easy process and that *meaning within people* cannot be overlooked.

Loneliness – Loneliness is a universal malady. It is no respecter of persons. It is a common occurrence for many. Because of its seriousness, loneliness does need a remedy. It needs to be overcome and there are professional helps, caring groups, and practical guidelines that can be found and utilized.

Maps – Maps are visualization tools for giving distinct directions or providing spatial data. There are many different types of maps available.

Melody – Melody is designed to command attention. Technically, it is a series of measured and accented tones meant to inspire and produce imaginative creativity. It is enhanced by *harmony* and *rhythm*.

Moral Compass – The compass is a much-needed and frequently-used instrument for navigational purposes in land, sea or the air. It can be highly sophisticated and used for multiple purposes. The term *moral compass* is reference to our staying on course with regard to our moral practices and spiritual values.

Names – Language matters and names are important! They give identification, a sense of power, authority and reputation. They communicate something of the character of the individual named.

Nice Guy – Nice guys do not have to finish last. Case in point is Arnold Palmer, the world's "King of Golf" and a champion in many ways. His own philosophy of life was strengthened by what he identified as the ability to "always reach within oneself to bring out the best." He is indeed Mr. Nice Guy.

Oh, Really? – This expression points toward a credibility gap between our speech and our actions. In the final analysis, it is an issue of *integrity*. A person with integrity is a "whole" person who avoids duplicity, hypocrisy, manipulation and rationalization.

Oops! – This is a verbal exclamation used to designate that a mistake has been made or a failure has occurred.

Quantum Thinking – It points to creative thought processes that challenges basic assumptions, triggers insights, breaks habits, changes mental models or paradigms, rearranges cognitive activities, and projects outside the conventional realms of logical thoughts and reasoned structures.

Purposes – Purposes refer to design, not something that happens accidentally. To be purposeful is to aim resolutely at a specific goal. Intending, resolving and planning are part of the process when considering purposes.

Repetition – Repetition takes place when that which is said, made, done, or happens again, or again and again, occurs. It may happen to a student who has to take over a course he or she has failed to pass. It may refer to a person who has been convicted a number of times for criminal activity or violating the law. It may reference a rebroadcast of a radio or television program. This list of repetitive instances could continue *ad infinitum*. When repetition occurs over and over it is often called *reiteration*.

Results – Achievements emerges from a simple formula that could lead to a complicated interactional pattern. That formula, which gives exponential results, is: *Motivations* times *Abilities* times *Opportunities* equals *Achievements*.

Rock Formations – Rock formations may mean different things to different people. To the musician it is a combination of many sounds with a hurried beat that may be accompanied by outlandish expressions of sexuality. To the geologist it generally means a scientific study of the development and structure of the earth's crust with various rock types. To Christians, it concerns the Lord Jesus Christ and His followers with specific attention to the strength, reliability and of God's character and functioning abilities.

Secular Humanism – *Secularism* is a system of doctrines and practice that either disregards or totally rejects any form of religious faith and worship. It wants no intrusion of religion into the affairs of state or public life. *Humanism* is a modern, non-theistic, and rationalistic movement that adheres to the belief that man is capable by himself of self-fulfillment without any dependence on supernatural interference. Placed together, these concepts produce a *secular humanist*.

Serendipity – This beautiful word refers to the fortunate facility for making happy chance discoveries. The concept of *serendipity* is borrowed from the Persian fairy tale, *The Three Princes of Serendip*. The term was coined by Horace Walpole in 1743. Serendip was an ancient word for Ceylon, now Sri Lanka.

Simple – In a brief explanation, it means "life expression in unhurried and unsophisticated fashion." It's as *simple* as that.

Small Things – This is a phrase often used to describe those aspects of our lives that are of minor importance or consequence.

Tomorrow – This is a popular theme in life and in lyrics for music. It points to the future and often features the unknown.

Under the Radar – This is a term employed to indicate a prearranged and predetermined attempt to avoid detection so as to escape danger, destruction, or punishment of some sort.

Up for Grabs – The slang expression, "up for grabs" has the positive meaning of something that is freely available, ready to be taken. It is out in the open and waiting to be grabbed by anyone who wants it. From the negative viewpoint, this phrase means doubt, wavering, vacillating, hesitating, fluctuating, questioning, to have mental reservations. Fears and degrees of apprehension are also factors involved.

What Say You? – I'm sure that you recognize this expression as the *theme* for each of the chapters of this book. It is an attempt to invite reader participation in the thinking and expressive processes regarding each of the topics presented. It is designed to personalize the approach, and to expand the concepts that are introduced. It tests the abilities to communicate shared messages and understandings. It invited evaluative dialogue in an empathic setting with no risks involved. Happily, these purposes will be accomplished.